Practical Parenting Tips

Vicki Lansky

Meadowbrook Press
Deephaven, Minnesota 55391

Special thanks go to Kathryn Ring, editor of PRACTICAL PARENTING newsletter, for her help in editing this book.

Cover illustration by Lynn Johnston. Text illustrations, also by Lynn Johnston, originally appeared in David, We're Pregnant!; Hi Mom! Hi Dad!; Do They Ever Grow Up?; and Watch Me Grow: a Baby Memory and Record Book.

Editor: Kathryn Ring
Asst. Editor: Mary Holm.

Designer: Terry Dugan
Production Manager: John Ware

Library of Congress Cataloging in Publication Data

Lansky, Vicki.
  Practical parenting tips.

  Includes index.
    1. Children — Management — Handbooks, manuals, etc.
  2. Infants — Care and hygiene — Handbooks, manuals,
  etc. I. Title. II. Title: Practical parenting tips
  HQ769.L245   649'.1   80-18646
  ISBN 0 915658-69-0 (pb)
  ISBN 0 915658-70-4 (hc)

Printed in the United States of America.

Introduction

My first child had the good grace to arrive at the end of May, so I was able to wheel him to the park almost daily. For him there was the fresh air and sunshine — for me there were the other new mothers on the park bench. It did not take me long to discover that their babies, took revised their waking schedules nightly and were fussy in the evenings when adults longed for private time. To my relief, I found I didn't have the only child who hadn't read Dr. Spock!

Not only did I get support from these park bench mothers — I got a lot of ideas from them. These weren't the kind of ideas I read in babycare books or heard in the pediatrician's office. They were practical tips born in experience, so they seemed worth trying. Other mothers, I was finding, were a wonderful source of information.

Several years later I put together two cookbooks, FEED ME I'M YOURS and THE TAMING OF THE C.A.N.D.Y. MONSTER. Both were collections of recipes and feeding ideas that had worked for me and other mothers. I am not a nutrition expert, but I do know what is good for my kids and in what forms they will eat it. I simply shared what I felt were good ideas. The success of these two books continues to amaze me.

In 1979 I began publishing a newsletter called PRACTICAL PARENTING because I still wanted to know more about what was working for other parents. Each issue of the newsletter includes a place for readers to answer questions posed by other parents. We ask parents to share their questions, recipes, tips and experiences. So from the tips sent in to the newsletter, from word of mouth ("the mothers' network"), from my experiences, from sources of all kinds, I have collected the the best of childcare tips that parents have shared for the first five years of living with small children.

Vicki

P.S. And now, a revision of the first edition of PRACTICAL PARENTING TIPS, made necessary because of the over 200 great new tips I've received (and felt I had to share!) from readers of the first edition and of the newsletter.

Acknowledgements

My special thanks to the thousands of PRACTICAL PARENTING newsletter subscribers who have taken the time to share tips, hints and ideas that have worked for them and to contributors, too numerous to list here, who sent me tips after reading the first edition of PRACTICAL PARENTING TIPS.

Thanks also to the scores of parents who responded to surveys, participated in focus group panels and read the manuscript of the first edition in its various stages. They sifted through the collection of tips, adding ... even subtracting ... and revising as needed.

Abigail F. Farber, M.D.

Vivian Adkins
Sharon Amastae
Susan Anderson
Kenneth Andreas
Cathy Andrews
Carol Andruskiewicz
Marcia Ashodian
Beverly Audeh
Gayle and Clifford Baker
Chester Ball, Jr.
Chris Baumgartner
Sarah Bell
Jeanne Blasi
Carrie Bloedel
Barbara Bowen
Eric Bowman
Maureen Bozicevich
Beadie Cambardella
Marjorie Cargill
Eric Carroll
Nancy and
    Thomas Caswell
Francie Conley
Marcia Conley
Mrs. M. Cooper
Donna and
    Dan Counselman
Gay Courter
Jill and John DeGutis
Bessie Dobbs
Gail Dodge
Beth Dooley
Gail Duke
Kay Dyer
Carol Eggers
Karen and
    Lawrence Evans
Linda and Robert Fegan
Jerome Fishkin
Linda Fornelli
Debbie and
    Glenn Freeman
Shirley Gayer
Sandra Gingrich

Mrs. Ivan Grabhorn
Emily Grainger
Kathe Grooms
Marlene Gwiazdon
Jerry Hallfin
Mary Beth Hamann
Merrie Ann Handley
Roberta Heeson
Fritz Heger
Eileen Helm
Gilda Henderson
Rhonda Hendrickson
Sharon Herpers
Diana Hestwood
Jeanne Hill
Jackie Hofhenke
Kay Hunke
Karen Jenkins
Susan Jones
Winnie Jones
Becky Kajander
Linda Kapler
Elaine Kaskela
Carol Keich
Jan Kendig
Mary Ann Koenigsfeld
Nancy Kress
Diane Kruck
Joan Lake
Richard Larson
Mary Jane Leenstra
Melodee and
    Maury Lewin
Joyce Lewis
Susan Lipke
Froma Lippman
Sue Ludwil
Roberta Majors
Gary Manuell
Jill Marks
Debbie McDaniel
Margy McManus

Harriet Meehan
Deborah Megginson
Kathy Mellott
Mrs. John Miller
Sandi Mink
Edna Moon
Ann Morris
Camelia Nocella
Karen Olness, M.D.
Jean Pierre
Pam Pierre
Wynann Plocher
Catherine and
    William Poulos
Kyla Reed
Phoebe Resnick
Judy Roth
Victoria Rule
John Runkle
Stanton Samenow
Sharon Schaaf
Jerry Schiller
Deidre and Ray Schipani
Cindy Schreiner
Norene and
    Richard Schulenberg
Donna Schwartz
Cyndy Schwenk
Colleen Shaskin
Bonnie Silvera
Ronna Sittig
Deborah Smollen
Marietta Spencer
Beverly Spindler
Sheila Steiner
Cynda Thompson
Melissa Thun
Linda Trust
Gail Weiner
Sherry Weinstein
Judy Winterhalter
Karen Woods
Julie Yoder
Sandi Zimlich

Contents

1. New Baby Care

2. Child Care: the Basics

3. Hygiene and Health

4. Coping with Kids at Home

5. The Challenge of Parenting

6. Family Heritage

7. Families on the Go

8. Child's Play

9. Special Situations

Chapter 1

New Baby Care

Having a baby is not unlike entering a tunnel. We can't see the end and we wonder what we have gotten ourselves into! We emerge five years later, having had less sleep than we might have wished, but thinking that it wasn't that rough, after all. The difficult days become difficult to remember.

Despite the newness of everything we must do, it doesn't really take long to become old hands at baby care. Though babies don't arrive with attached instructions, they do express their needs loud and clear. And as far as our expertise is concerned, new babies don't realize that everything we do first time 'round is just as new for us as it is for them ... WHEW!

YOUR NEW BABY AND YOU

Amid the flurry that follows the birth of a baby, it's important to remember that everyone has adjustments to make. If it's your first child, "Mom" and "Dad" are new roles to be tried out. If there are siblings in the house, their positions in the family are changed — overnight!

Along with the excitement and pride that follow a birth come stress and fatigue. We're apt to demand more of ourselves than we do of those around us, but taking care of yourself adequately will make you better able to help everybody else deal with the adjustments. It's a time for spouses to be very good to each other and to put off big decisions, if possible.

- Find the "Do Not Disturb" sign from your honeymoon and use it on your front door. Or make a sign: "Ssssh! Baby and Mommy are resting!"

- Disconnect the phone when you don't want to answer it (if you take it off the hook, dial 0 and jam a pencil in the dial to hold it, to avoid the buzzing sound), or install phone silencer switches.

- Let modern technology help you avoid answering the phone when you don't want to. Record the details of your baby's birth on a telephone answering machine and add a message about when is the best time to call.

- Make some part of every day special, for spouses only, whether it's a late dinner together, a walk around the block or only a five-minute noontime telephone call.

- GET OUT, alone or as a couple, on some kind of regular basis. If that's absolutely impossible, at least look for a movie theater that offers a "crying room" so that you can enjoy a show in a soundproof area where you won't have to worry about the baby disturbing others.

- Don't worry if you don't feel overwhelming love for your infant instantly. It often takes some time, maybe months, for real parental love to develop. Relax — enjoy the developing bond between you and your baby.

- Find some support, be it a single friend who also has a new baby or an organized group.

FEEDING YOUR BABY

A baby's stomach is about the size of its fist — taking in a lot of milk at one time just isn't possible. No wonder infants spend so much time eating!

If you're breastfeeding, the first rule is to relax. Find a quiet place, away from distractions and visitors, for your first feedings. And don't watch the clock — the baby doesn't. If the father feels a bit left out, remember that there are things he CAN do, such as changing and bathing the baby and bringing it to the big bed for night feedings. Some parents decide to give the baby one bottle of formula a day, both to help involve Dad and to let Mom get some needed sleep or a chance to get out of the house. If you use powdered infant formula, it's easy to mix up just one bottle at a time.

Support for the Nursing Mother

Contact the La Leche League International (9616 Minneapolis Avenue, Franklin Park, IL 60131, 312-455-7730) for information about the local group in your area. Women interested in the breastfeeding of infants have joined to provide information and support for one another.

Dressing comfortably for breastfeeding

- Take a front-buttoning nightgown or one with concealed slits with you to the hospital.

- Wear a stretch bra, if you like, which can simply be lifted up for nursing. Some women buy bras before they go to the hospital, getting a size larger (and a CUP size larger) than they wore during pregnancy, but this isn't right for everyone. Perhaps best is to buy a bra extender in a sewing notions department for the extra "give" you may need.

- Try using a man's soft handkerchief in your bra cup to prevent leaks from coming through, or use about four layers of an old knitted undershirt or stitched-together two- to three-inch circles of terrycloth. Or cut a heavy sanitary napkin or diaper to fit. (And of course there are commercially available nursing pads or other products.)

- Remember that printed tops will make stains less visible if you do leak.

- Unbutton front-buttoning blouses from the bottom for modest nursing. Or wear a knit pullover; the baby's head will cover your bare midriff, and the pullover will cover your breast.

- Keep a loose-fitting cardigan handy and don't overlook the quick cover-up possibilities of ponchos, scarves or receiving blankets.

Nursing techniques

- Protect linens and blankets, when you nurse in bed, by covering them with a crib-sized waterproof protector.

- Use a big bed pillow with arms for nursing in bed.

- Wrap up in a big blanket or get into a snuggle sack with the baby in the winter if you sit up to nurse at night. Milk flows better if you're warm and cozy.

- Select a cushioned rocker, armchair or sofa for nursing when you're up, one with low arms to rest your own arms on, and put a pillow under your nursing arm. If you're buying a rocker, remember that a wooden one will be easier to keep clean than an upholstered one.

- Put the baby on a pillow on your lap; you may find that doing so puts him or her at just the right level for comfort.

- Keep track of which breast you used last by transferring a safety pin from one side of your bra strap to the other. Or buy a light-weight expandable bracelet and slip it from one wrist to the other. Or use a ring that is loose enough to transfer easily from hand to hand. You may want to start on the right side each morning; you'll be able to remember how many times you've fed the baby and work it out. Most mothers start nursing with the breast used LAST.

- Put your finger in the corner of the baby's mouth to break the suction and ease him or her off your breast, when you want to stop nursing.

- If the baby falls asleep, change the diaper to help wake him or her when you're ready to change breasts.

- Wear a bright "necklace" of colored wooden beads or ribbons for your baby to look at while you're nursing.

- Be aware that some babies find it hard to settle down against slippery nylon or polyester. If you're wearing a shirt or top of either fabric, slip a diaper or receiving blanket between yourself and the baby.

- Try expressing milk in a warm shower or bath if you're engorged and the baby isn't ready to nurse. Experiment with all types of breast pumps; they don't all work for everyone.

Bottle-feeding

It's understood today that a baby's food needn't be really warm, but it goes against the grain for some parents to serve up a cold bottle. A fancy electric bottle warmer isn't necessary, though. Take the chill off in any way you wish, and use the time while the bottle's heating to change the baby. Test the temperature of the formula by squirting a drop or two onto your wrist; if it feels comfortably warm, it's right for the baby.

While it isn't critical for development, some parents hold their babies in one arm for one feeding, the other for the next, to help the infants develop good eye muscle coordination.

- Warm a bottle by standing it in a couple of inches of water in an electric coffee maker for a few minutes, by setting it in any handy bowl, pan or mug of hot water or by running hot tap water over it. Shake the bottle occasionally to warm formula evenly.

- Stand an uncapped eight-ounce bottle in your microwave at high power for 15 to 30 seconds if it's at room temperature and for 30 to 60 seconds if it's cold from the refrigerator.

- Keep extra formula in the refrigerator to add to a too-warm bottle.

- Make middle-of-the-night feedings easier by taking a COLD (from the refrigerator) bottle to your room or the baby's when you go to bed. It will probably warm to room temperature by the time you need it.

- Regulate the flow of formula by loosening the bottle collar if the flow is too slow, tightening it if the flow is too fast.

- Hold the bottle at feeding angle to check the nipple hole size. If formula comes out in steady, even drops, the nipple is ready for use.

- Let your baby use bottle straws; formula will flow evenly no matter what position the bottle is in.

The business of bottles

- Store bottles in the refrigerator in an empty six-pack bottle holder to keep them together and safe from tipping. Or make and store formula in a sterilized glass coffee pot.

- Boil nipples in water in a glass jar in the microwave oven to clean them. A teaspoonful of vinegar in the water will prevent hard water deposits in the jar.

- Enlarge nipple holes, if necessary, by putting toothpicks in them and boiling the nipples for three minutes, or by sticking a very hot needle into the rubber a few times. If the hole is too big, TOSS the nipple and start using the extras you bought!

- Rinse out empty bottles as soon as possible or you'll find "cottage cheese" in them later. Shake a bottle filled with warm water with dry rice in it to scrub out milk rings. To get rid of a sour-milk smell, fill bottles with warm water, add a teaspoon of baking soda, shake well and let stand overnight.

- Remove juice stains by putting baking soda in warm water in the bottle and scrubbing with a bottle brush. If juice pulp clogs the nipple, cover the top of the bottle with a piece of cheesecloth to strain it out.

- Wash bottles in the dishwasher, if you have one. They won't need sterilizing.

Burping

Don't worry if your baby doesn't always burp after a feeding, especially if you're breastfeeding. If he or she seems comfortable after you've given it a good try, forget it. Do be careful not to "pat" too hard; you may cause the baby to vomit. Some parents find it better to use a gentle upward stroke instead of patting.

- Put your baby on your shoulder with a diaper underneath and gently pat his or her back between the shoulder blades.

- Tie a bib around YOUR neck if you get tired of a diaper, and switch the bib from shoulder to shoulder as you switch the baby.

- Lay the baby on your lap, tummy down, with his or her head turned a little to the side. Pat or gently rub, from the bottom up.

- Make a "horseshoe" with your thumb and index finger and put the baby's chin into it as he or she "sits" on your lap, leaning against your arm. Pat or stroke upward.

- Put your hand under the baby's sternum and lean the baby toward your palm (draped with cloth or diaper), while firmly but gently rubbing his or her back.

- Squeeze the baby's back gently, while the baby is on your shoulder or in your lap, beginning at the kidney area and working slowly up to the shoulders.

PUTTING YOUR BABY TO SLEEP

Some babies sleep for long stretches of time, others catnap through the 24 hours, and many seem to prefer sleeping through the day rather than the night. A new baby sleeping through the night is the exception, not the rule, whatever your friends and relatives may say. During the first three to six months, parents usually have to adjust their own sleeping habits to the baby's, or take shifts, to avoid exhaustion. (And, in fact, one definition of a parent is "a person who is no longer EVER guaranteed a full night's sleep!")

Inducing sleep

Sometimes babies need a little time to cry or fuss before sleeping. You'll soon know if the crying means something serious. Your first thought will be for the baby's comfort. Position him or her on side or stomach first — some say sleeping on the back is best avoided to prevent newborns from gagging on milk they may spit up.

It's not necessary or practical to try to live in a silent house. If you maintain a reasonable level of noise, the baby will become accustomed to it. You may wish to play a radio softly just outside the baby's room. (But if you find that the shrill ring of the phone does wake the baby, put a pad under the phone; a thick potholder works nicely.) Remember that giving the baby a feeling of security is the most important thing.

- Establish a "sleep routine" from the beginning, especially if you'll be traveling or expecting the baby to sleep in different places. Sing the same lullaby every time and rub a special spot, perhaps the back of the head or the forehead, and rub that spot at sleep time ONLY.

- Attach springs to the bottoms of the crib legs and try rocking the baby to sleep.

- Spray the bassinet sheets very lightly with the same perfume you used in the hospital and it will seem to your baby that you are near.

- Try confining the baby gently, bundling him or her lightly in a receiving blanket. Some babies sleep better with a rather firm swaddling, reminiscent of the pre-birth environment.

- Place the baby on his or her side. Roll up two receiving blankets and put one roll along the baby's neck, the other along the stomach. Tuck in snugly.

- Position the baby in a corner of the crib or bassinet with his or her head touching the bumper or soft padding to provide a feeling of security. This also allows you to move the baby from corner to corner if the sheet gets wet or soiled.

- Let the baby sleep upright occasionally, if he or she prefers it, using an infant seat or carrying him or her in a soft fabric front carrier.

- Slip a warm heating pad or hot water bottle onto the sheet when you take the baby up for a feeding so that the bed will be warm when you return him or her to it (but then take pad or bottle out). Or warm a blanket in the dryer while you feed the baby, if that's convenient.

- Tape record the sound of a running dishwasher or of water filling the tub and play it to lull a child to sleep. The sound of running water simulates intrauterine sounds.

- Or invest in the rather expensive electronic teddy bear which also duplicates intrauterine sounds. Start using it right from the beginning, say parents who like it.

When the baby confuses day and night

This phenomenon is often associated with colic. If the father works outside and the mother stays home, it's logical that she bear the brunt, but she MUST catch up on her sleep during the day, whenever the baby naps. If both work, they must share the nighttime discomfort.

- Try to keep the baby awake during the early evening to encourage the swing to nighttime sleep. Keep the baby slightly cool and upright in infant seat or carrier. Talk, sing, dance or do whatever will stimulate the baby.

- Add a little cereal to the last evening bottle for a meal a bit more substantial.

- Change bathtime to just before bedtime so the baby will be relaxed.

- Give night feedings in dim light so the baby will realize that they're different from daytime feedings.

- Avoid too many visitors and too much handling of the baby by strangers, which can overstimulate the baby and make sleep difficult.

- Allow yourself a good cry! This, too, will pass.

Making night checking easier

- Put a dimmer on the light switch.

- Keep a soft night light burning in the baby's room.

- Use a flashlight; keep it near your bed.

- Apply petroleum jelly or vegetable oil to the side rails of the crib to keep them from squeeking when they're raised or lowered. Or rub them with waxed paper.

Keeping your baby cozy

- Test for comfort by gently touching the back of the baby's neck. (Be sure your hand is not cold; warm it next to your body or under hot water first if necessary.) If the baby's neck is warm, he or she is comfortable. If it's damp, the baby may be too warm. Arms and legs can also give a hint as to the baby's comfort, and you can check for a pink or rosy color. Don't go by the feeling of the baby's hands — they usually feel cool.

- Use blanket sleepers of various weights, depending on the season, and skip a blanket altogether. If you're really worried about the baby being cold, put on two sets of sleepers, but be sure they don't bind and cut off circulation.

- Use a rubberized flannel "lap pad" over crib sheets, or spread a diaper across the sheet, to avoid having to disturb the baby by changing sheets after every leak and spit-up.

WHEN YOUR BABY CRIES

Babies cry and fuss for a variety of reasons, but you'll soon be able to "translate" the cry of distress. Obvious solutions are available for many cries, including those of discomfort from being too cool or too warm, simple boredom or relief of tension. One classic check that parents make concerns the open safety pin; another common check is for the tiny thread on the inside of a garment (or even a thread from the bassinet skirting), tangled around a baby's hand or foot and HURTING. Experienced parents check carefully and clip all such threads.

Sometimes, a baby just cries . . . and cries . . . and cries . . . and you know there's nothing wrong, no physical reason for it. Don't feel guilty — the baby isn't crying because you're a "bad" parent —there's nothing personal in it!

20 Ways to Cope with Crying

1. Walk or dance with the baby. Try dancing to different kinds of music.
2. Rock the baby.
3. Bounce the baby gently in your arms or on a bed. A water bed is especially soothing.
4. Take the baby for a ride in the carriage or the car.
5. Put the baby in a wind-up swing.
6. Turn up the music on the radio or stereo, run the vacuum or a hair dryer.
7. Offer the baby a "noisy" toy; shake it, rattle it.
8. Sing or talk to the baby in a quiet, sing-song way.
9. Carry the baby with you about the house in a soft front carrier, close to your body.
10. Lay the baby tummy down across your lap and gently rub his or her back.
11. Lay the baby across a warm hot-water bottle on your lap or a bed.
12. Massage the baby's body and limbs gently; use a warmed lotion, if the weather is cool.
13. Swaddle the baby tightly.
14. Feed and burp the baby one more time. Or offer a little warm water. In desperation, add a tiny bit of sugar to the water or to weak camomile tea.
15. Offer a pacifier (the Nuk allows less air to pass in around the baby's mouth and so is better for a colicky baby) and hold it in the baby's mouth if necessary.
16. Or let the baby suck the top third of your little finger (turning your nail down so it won't poke the roof of the baby's mouth if he or she sucks hard).
17. Hold the baby close and breathe slowly and calmly; the baby may feel your calmness and become quiet.
18. Cross the baby's arms across the chest and hold him or her down on a bed with a gentle, firm pressure.
19. Remove yourself and let someone else take over for awhile. If a family member is not available, consider hiring a sitter for a short period of time.
20. If NOTHING works, put the baby in his or her bed, close the door and turn up the TV or radio. Take a shower to drown the noise and to relax yourself. Check the child every 15 minutes or so, for your own peace of mind.

Colic

Colic is not a disease; it can't be tested for. It's a symptom of severe cramps of the digestive tract. The baby pulls the legs up, clenches the fists and often flushes bright red. Crying may go on for hours, often in the late afternoon and evening. Fortunately, colic rarely lasts past the third month of a child's life, but until it's over, it's hard on both baby and parents.

In a breastfed baby, colic may be caused by a reaction to something in the mother's diet. She may try avoiding such things as strong-flavored foods and drinks that contain caffeine. A recent discovery is that some babies are allergic to milk and other dairy products that their mothers drink or eat. A change to a soy formula that does not contain corn syrup or corn solids often helps colicky babies, too. Consult your doctor before you make a change.

- Try to handle and feed the baby calmly. A parent's tension may be transmitted to the baby and cause stress that brings on colic.

- Try burping the baby BEFORE starting a feeding to prevent a bubble from being trapped at the bottom of the stomach. And burp the baby several times during a feeding.

- Use plastic bottle liners for a bottle-fed baby. The baby will swallow less air if the air is first squeezed out of the bag, and this will lessen abdominal discomfort. The Nuk nipple is also good — it lets in less air than some others do.

- Feed the baby in as nearly an upright position as possible. The bubble at the bottom of the baby's stomach will rise toward the top of the food and be burped easily, preventing the pain of trapped gas.

- Mix equal amounts of 7-Up and water in a three-ounce bottle and give it to a colicky baby between feedings to help him or her pass gas.

- Let the baby suck a peppermint candy stick or melt a small piece of the candy in water and give it in a bottle. Peppermint often has a soothing effect.

- Or lay the baby in the crib on his or her back, pull the left arm and right leg gently, then the right arm and left leg, to relieve gas.

KEEPING YOUR BABY CLEAN

You won't be giving your baby a full bath until the umbilical cord falls off. Even then, remember that babies don't really get dirty, except for their bottoms, faces and necks. First babies probably get bathed more than others, simply because parents have more time than they do with two or more children. A day without a bath is NOT a disgrace; skipping a day, or even several days, may be best for both you and the baby. On the other hand, when you both feel the need of relaxation, a long, warm tub bath together may ease tension. You'll soon learn the best time of day for baths; immediately following a meal is best for some, but not for all.

Try not to be nervous when you bathe your baby the first few times. Relax and enjoy it, and the process will soon become routine. Make sure everything you need is within reach before starting, and try using only a little water in the tub until you become confident.

Bath equipment

- Make do at first with a plastic dishpan on the kitchen counter or bathroom vanity.

- Bathe the newborn in an inflatable baby tub. Or, with the larger plastic tub, use a sculptured foam liner.

- Or bathe the baby in the bathroom or kitchen sink, if the faucet is placed so that he or she is not likely to bump against it. Be careful when the baby begins to kick — his or her head may bump against the side of the sink.

- Clip a large towel around your own neck, like a bib. It will keep you dry during the bath and give you an instant wrap-up for the baby.

Bathing routines

- Run the cold water last in a sink so that if the baby touches the faucet it won't be hot and burn him or her.

- Use even mild baby soap sparingly to preserve the baby's own protective skin oils; soap is often responsible for skin rashes.

- Put a bit of cold cream or petroleum jelly on the baby's brows to channel soap away from his or her eyes.

- Set the plastic bottle of lotion or shampoo in the tub with the baby and it will be warm when you're ready for it.

- Prevent cradle cap by combing even a bald head daily. Shampoo often and use a soft bristle brush or soft toothbrush (the long handle provides good maneuverability).

- Treat cradle cap by smearing on baby oil or petroleum jelly at night and washing it off in the morning with a soapy washcloth. Or try a paste of baking soda and water.

- Put any powder you use into your hand first, away from the baby's face, so that powder in the air isn't inhaled by the baby. And for the same reason, don't let an older baby play with an open powder container.

Preventing diaper rash

Experienced parents may smile a bit at the thought of "preventing" diaper rash. It seems that almost every baby has it, to some degree, at one time or another.

- Give the baby warm, soapy baths, with mild soap. Or sprinkle a little Dreft in the water when you clean the diaper area — it's germicidal.

- Mix powder in equal amounts with cornstarch to save money and still have the fresh baby powder odor plus extra protection from wetness.

- Don't use plastic pants, which hold moisture in — but be prepared to change the baby often and to accumulate inordinate amounts of laundry.

- Consider disposables, if you've been using cloth diapers. Some, but not all, babies who wear disposables seem less apt to have diaper rash.

- Don't use fabric softener with every diaper wash. Babies are often sensitive to softener buildup (and overuse makes diapers less absorbent).

Treating diaper rash

Once the baby has diaper rash, you try one thing ... and then another. Many doctors oppose "greasing" a baby with oils and lotions, and experienced parents don't use any solutions or ointments too thickly — "more is better" doesn't apply here.

- Smooth on vegetable shortening; it's cheaper than commercial preparations and usually works as well. Petroleum jelly, at about the same cost, is also good. (Store it in a plastic squeeze bottle to make it easier to handle.)

- Or "toast" regular flour in the oven and smooth it on the rash.

- Try applying zinc oxide or a paste of cornstarch and water. (Current opinion is mixed as to the advisability of using cornstarch alone, however.)

- Let the baby stay naked or at least bare-bottomed as often as possible — a light case of diaper rash may be air/sun-cured quickly.

- Dry the baby's bottom with a hair dryer set at "warm" and held at least six inches from the skin.

- You may find an over-the-counter preparation that works. If serious diaper rash persists, check with your doctor for a prescription.

DIAPERING

Don't worry if you missed the Red Cross course in diapering. Mothers quickly become expert and not only CAN but DO change diapers in their sleep — fathers, too. Disposables are easiest to use, and you can save money on them by buying by the case, when they're on sale. Whatever your final choice will be, disposables are great for the first few weeks, when you need to save your energy. Cloth diapers are cheaper in the long run and ecologically more satisfying to some. If you have two in diapers, you'll find a diaper service cheaper than disposables and certainly more convenient than doing your own.

Cleaning bottoms

Some parents like the convenience of pre-moistened towelettes for cleaning babies' bottoms, but there are lots of alternatives.

- Make your own inexpensive wipes by thoroughly soaking a roll of toilet tissue (the strong kind — not extra soft) in baby oil in a shallow bowl. Pull out the center core and start the roll from the middle. Store in a plastic bag or covered container.

- Keep a roll of toilet paper or a package of tissues at the dressing area for cleanups.

- Or use Handiwipes; they rinse out easily.

- Or try torn-up old cloth diapers, which you can toss in the washer with the other cloth diapers.

- Wipe a soiled bottom clean with oil on a cotton ball.

- Try changing diapers on the bathroom vanity. Lay the baby on a towel, hold legs up, and scoot his or her bottom to the edge of the sink for hand splashing and cleaning.

- Color code washcloths, if you use them for cleanup: one color for the bath, one for diapering.

Diapering

- Fold the plastic top of a disposable diaper down to the inside to prevent the "wicking" that soaks wetness up into other clothing.

- Keep a roll of masking tape handy to mend torn tabs on disposables and to mend plastic pants.

- Try using disposables with elastic around the legs to prevent leaks. Tiny babies' legs aren't plump enough to allow for snug closings.

- Cover an infant boy's penis with your hand or a cloth as you expose it, to avoid being squirted. Point it down when you fasten the diaper to head the stream where you want it.

- Cut just what you need from a roll of gauze to cover a circumcision. The roll is less expensive than pre-cut squares and works as well or better.

Diaper pins

DIAPER pins with plastic-covered ends are what you want — not ordinary safety pins. Always place your fingers between the baby's skin and the diaper to prevent sticking him or her with a pin.

- Snap a wrist pincushion around the top rung of the crib or dressing table as a diaper pin holder when the baby is tiny. It's not a safe procedure when a child is old enough to reach for it. Or stick pins in a thick potholder or hang closed pins on a cup hook screwed into the wall.

- Stick pins in a bar of soap, with paper wrapping left on to contain flakes, to make them slide through cloth easily. Or stick them in a decorative candle for attractive storage.

- Run pins through a strand of your hair or across the top of your head to make them go through cloth easily.

- Attach a few diaper pins to your key chain so that you'll always have extras handy when you're away from home.

- Don't EVER hold pins in your mouth — babies are great imitators!

Making the dressing area convenient

You may find it practical to set up a "satellite" dressing area to save steps. Keep it stocked with diapers, clothing and duplicates of other essential items. Or keep baby supplies in a clean plastic garden carry-all and take it about the house with you. Try to make the main dressing area light and bright, but consider installing a dimmer on the light for nighttime changing.

- Use the top of a dresser for a changing table. Cut an old belt in half and staple the ends to the top of the dresser to make a safety belt for the baby. Line the drawers with wrapping paper from your baby shower gifts to make them attractive.

- Cover your changing table pad with a pillowcase, which can be removed and laundered easily.

- Hang a shelf above the changing table to hold necessities and to keep them up out of reach of toddlers in the house.

- Or make or buy a wall hanging (about two feet square) with pockets to fit small articles into. It can be hung with curtain rods top and bottom.

- Keep a thermos of warm water near the changing table at night for quick cleanups. You'll avoid stumbling around in the dark and running the water for what seems hours to get the right temperature.

- Save time by folding diapers only as you need them. Keep a laundry basket of clean, unfolded diapers near the dressing area.

- Keep two diaper pails at the dressing area: one (smallish and, for cloth diapers, half filled with water to which borax has been added so that it won't get smelly) for soiled diapers, the other for wet or soiled clothing that will later be transferred to the laundry.

- Cut down on cleaning chores by using plastic liners inside the diaper pail.

BABY LAUNDRY

It's unbelievable to new parents that ONE TINY PERSON can generate so much laundry — and it's always a surprise, even to those who have gone through it more than once. If you use cloth diapers, you want them not only clean but also germ-free, to help prevent diaper rash.

Diapers

- Rinse out diapers, even those that are only wet, before putting them in the diaper pail. Empty soiled diapers in the toilet.

- Sprinkle a little baking soda in the diaper pail to keep diapers from souring.

- Soak diapers overnight in the washing machine with soap and a commercial soaking solution. Run them through the regular cycle the next day, then run once more without soap for a good rinse.

- Or soak in a plastic bag in the diaper pail with water to which about a cup of borax has been added.

- Add a handful of baking soda to the next-to-the-last rinse to keep the diapers soft and fresh-smelling. Fabric softener is expensive and may cause skin irritation.

- Or try another old-fashioned diaper softener and whitener — vinegar. A cupful in the second rinse gets rid of soap, too, and helps prevent diaper rash.

Plastic pants

- Dry plastic pants on the hangers of a multiple skirt hanger to avoid the heat of the dryer. Hang them in the sun to kill odors.

- Or dry them in the dryer, but use a softener or throw in a few towels.

- Rub a little baby oil into plastic pants that are becoming dry and brittle. Or try even putting the oil into the rinse water.

Stained clothes

- Soak stained clothes (or mildewed hand-me-downs) in hot water with a half-cup each of vinegar and laundry soap.

- Or soak overnight in hot water to which you add a cup each of laundry detergent, bleach and dishwasher detergent. Finish the wash cycle in the morning, run the clothes through a regular warm wash cycle and give them an extra rinse to be sure all chemicals are out of the fabric.

- Dab at soured dribbles on the baby's clothes with a moistened cloth dipped in baking soda.

Grab It and Run

Keep a pre-packed bag to grab as you go out the door with the baby. Stock it with diapers, an extra set of clothes, wipes, a light blanket and plastic bags (those that come in a roll are handy — always there!). A two-foot square of plastic or washable vinyl wallpaper can be put down anywhere for quick changes. Save the free samples of baby products you receive in the hospital for your traveling bag and keep the containers to refill with the contents of larger sizes. Keep a clean bottle set in the bag, with dry formula in it (or use it for water, if you're breastfeeding). You might also include a pillowcase to pop a blanket-wrapped baby into for snug warmth in winter and to keep a blanket from shedding on your clothes. And don't forget to restock your bag as soon as you return home from an outing.

A STIMULATING ENVIRONMENT

Gradually, your whole house will become baby- and child-oriented, but the baby's room will probably be the one most interesting to him or her. Remember that newborns can focus their eyes only on objects 7 to 12 inches away. By three months of age, a baby can focus well on more distant objects. Get down to your baby's level often, on a bed or the floor, so that you don't always look like a giant.

World within sight and sound

- Use as much color in the baby's room as you can, in paint, curtains and wall hangings. Buy or make a bright colored patchwork quilt; use printed sheets on the crib (regular double sheets, folded in half, work well — they can be very colorful and can be used later, on a big bed). Remember that infants see the colors red and yellow best and that faces, especially those with prominent eyes, are "readable" to them. Cheer yourself up and stimulate your baby by wearing bright, patterned clothes yourself.

- Sew a colorful fabric cover for a vinyl-covered crib bumper, both to protect the vinyl, which tears easily, and to make it more attractive.

- Decorate a wall with a montage of baby congratulation cards or frame some cards to hang separately. Or hang some cute plastic placemats.

- Fasten bright decals on the insides of the crib, bassinet or carriage.

- Put a colorful poster, kite or piece of wallpaper on the ceiling above the dressing table.

- Put a small cork board over the dressing table for an older child to display bright drawings for the baby.

- Keep a music box in the baby's room to appeal to the sense of sound, or hang wind chimes near a window that will be open in warm weather.

- Put your baby's infant seat on the floor, where he or she can see more. And put a mirror tile on the wall nearby — fun for your infant now and for your crawling child later.

- Hang some of the baby's toys and rattles on the crib with snap-on plastic shower curtain hooks. They're bright and strong; they keep toys in view and off the floor.

- Or attach small stuffed animals to the crib bumper with small pieces of Velcro.

- Decorate your baby's highchair with a colorful picture or decal, covered with two coats of polyethylene to make it permanent.

Mobiles

- Hang a mobile in the baby's room to encourage eye movement and awareness of surroundings, and remember that the baby will see the UNDERSIDE of it. Use FIRM cord — elastic is not safe for a reaching baby and a mobile on a thin string can fly away from a baby's reach or even be pulled down.

- Or let your older child construct a mobile for his or her new sibling. It could be made of butterflies cut from plastic meat trays, colored and strung with strong button thread or fishing line and tied to paper rods from coat hangers.

- Hang silver spoons from shoelaces for a mobile that sparkles and makes a charming, tinkling sound when it moves.

Social Life with Your Baby

Remember to serve only finger foods that can be eaten with one hand when you have a party with other parents and their new babies — everyone will have a baby on one arm!

SAVING MONEY ON EQUIPMENT

It's not necessary for parents to buy EVERY available piece of equipment for babies; there are many workable substitutes, especially during the first few months of an infant's life, when changes take place so quickly.

- Use a padded laundry basket or a car bed for a comfortable, portable in-house bed.

- Carry the baby's bathtub for sleeping away from home, or pad a deep dresser drawer for the baby to sleep in when you're visiting.

- Let a carriage serve as an infant bed. It can be gently rocked, as a crib can't.

- Substitute a small inflatable plastic wading pool for a playpen for a child who's not yet actively crawling.

- Consider propping your baby in a bean-bag chair occasionally instead of in an infant seat. The chair will be a practical addition to the child's room later, anyway.

YOUR BABY'S SIBLINGS

If there is an older child in your family, he or she will no doubt be excited at the prospect of a new baby. You'll want to talk about the baby, as it is, in Mommy's uterus, the way the child once was, and to let the child feel the baby's movements. And you'll want to talk about the baby as it will be — sleeping, crying, eating, taking a lot of Mommy's time. Be sure your older child doesn't expect an instant playmate!

Preparing the older sibling

- Move the older child up a step or two BEFORE the baby arrives — to a big bed from a crib, to another bedroom, to nursery school for a day or two a week — so that these changes won't be seen as rejections after the baby arrives.

- Invite another baby for a few visits to let your child see how things will be. You'll get a little practice, and the visiting baby's parents will OWE you.

- Take your child to the hospital, have lunch in the coffee shop and let the child help pick out a present for the baby and one for himself or herself. If possible, visit the nursery where the baby will be. This will be your chance to talk to your child about what will be happening to him or her while you're in the hospital.

- Take your child with you to a prenatal checkup to hear the baby's heartbeat, if your doctor's agreeable.

- Give the child a new baby doll to play with and care for, if he or she wants one.

- Involve Daddy actively. If he will be in charge of the older child at home, have him let the child know how happy he'll be when they spend that special time together.

- AND DON'T START ANY OF THIS TOO EARLY! The nine months may seem to go slowly for you, but for a child they are an eternity.

While you're gone

- Tape record some stories for your child to listen to while you're in the hospital.

- Leave a picture of yourself in your child's room.

- Prepare some little gifts to be handed out each day while you're gone.

- Send home little gifts from the hospital: flexible straws, packets of jelly, plastic cups.

- Ask your older child to take care of something special for you while you're in the hospital — perhaps a scarf or piece of jewelry.

- Call your child frequently from the hospital, especially if children are not allowed to visit on the maternity floor.

- Give the child at home a personal Polaroid snapshot of the new baby.

- Don't walk in carrying the baby on your return home, if possible; be prepared to devote a few minutes to your reunion with the older child.

Helping siblings deal with jealousy

It's important to understand that for your older child the trauma of a rival is very real. Jealousy may not appear until the baby is older and develops a real personality, but it's well to be prepared for it. You may want to allow any temporary regression of the older child to run its course with as little notice and comment as possible, while praising any particular grown-up behavior displayed. Don't expect the child to love the baby instantly. Make it clear that hurting the baby is not allowed, but that adoration is not required.

- Express your own occasional annoyance with the baby's demands to your older child, but not so often that he or she gets the idea that the new sibling is a permanent nuisance. Express your joy, too.

- Put a stool next to the baby's dressing table so that your older child can watch changing and dressing routines.

- Let the child help as much as possible with "our baby," holding, singing or talking to the baby and running errands around the house for you. Show your appreciation for the help.

- Set the baby's crib mattress at the lowest point so that an older child won't be able to try to pick him or her up.

- "Stall" visitors who come to see the baby so that the older child can be the center of attention for a few minutes. Show pictures of the child as well as of the baby. Then let the child help you show the baby off.

- Give the older child new privileges: a later bedtime, increased spending money or allowance, special things to do with a parent.

- Get out the older child's baby pictures, especially those that show you giving him or her the same kinds of attention you now give the baby.

- Have the baby bring the older child a gift from the hospital, perhaps a shirt that says, "I'm the big sister." Keep a few small surprise gifts on hand to give your older child when visitors bring gifts to the baby.

- Teach the older child that if he or she smiles often at the baby, the infant will soon return the smile. And show the child how to touch, love and cuddle the baby.

The Other Kind of "Sibling"

To help the family dog or cat adjust to the new baby, place a diaper or blanket with the baby at the hospital (make sure the staff knows your plan so it won't be washed). The day before the baby is brought home, give the cloth to the pet to play with and sniff — the baby's odor will then be a familiar one. You can "pet proof" the baby's room by putting a gate across the door; you'll still be able to see into the room and pets will be kept out.

YOUR BABY'S DOCTOR

Some parents question the need for routine checkups for healthy babies. But in the long run, they often save trouble and even money, because problems can be diagnosed early. A continuing medical history of a child is also often valuable if problems develop later in his or her life.

Seeing the doctor

- Keep a notepad in a convenient place in your home to make running notes of questions you want to ask at the checkup. Also note your baby's "history," including sleeping, crying and eating patterns, elimination habits and such.

- Don't be afraid to ask ANYTHING! A "foolish" question is better than a mistake.

- Make written notes of any verbal instructions the doctor or pediatric nurse practitioner gives you; what seems perfectly clear in the office may become less so by the time you get home.

- Save yourself trouble by having the baby wear a disposable diaper, even if you normally use cloth ones. You won't have to take a wet or soiled diaper home. And take masking tape with you so you can reuse the diaper if it's still dry.

Reasons to Call the Doctor

- The first occurrence of any illness new to the baby — even a cold.
- Diarrhea, when bowel movements are more watery and more frequent than usual.
- Blood-tinged urine or bowel movements.
- Poor feeding, when the baby stops the usual vigorous sucking during feedings.
- Unusual crying that continues, or a hoarse, husky cry.
- A significant change in the baby's usual color, breathing, behavior or activity.
- A rectal temperature of 101 degrees or higher.
- A listless, inactive attitude, if the baby is usually active and alert; or drowsiness at an unusual time, lasting a long time.
- Convulsions, "fits" or spells during which the child stiffens or twitches uncontrollably.
- Draining ears or ear pain, shown by constant turning of the head or pulling at the ear or crying when coughing.
- Forceful or projectile vomiting instead of the usual spitting up or cheesing.
- A "serious-looking" rash — one that covers a large part of the baby's body and is unfamiliar to you.
- Redness of or discharge from the baby's eyes.
- Any injury from which the pain or disability doesn't disappear within 15 minutes.

Chapter 2

Child Care: the Basics

The routines of feeding, clothing and getting your child to sleep move slowly from things you do for them to things you help them do themselves. While it often seems easier to do it all yourself, you'll want to encourage as much self-help as possible.

FEEDING

If you worry about "getting" the baby to eat — DON'T. It's not really possible. You can control the quality and variety that you offer, but the baby should control the quantity that's taken in. Be aware that a child's appetite usually decreases dramatically at about one year of age.

Try to make eating fun, and remember to monitor your own facial expression when feeding a child. Your wry face over the spinach will instantly trigger a negative reaction in the child.

Feeding the baby

- Warm baby food in an egg poacher, using the compartments for different foods.

- Use paper muffin cups for some appropriate baby foods and save dishwashing.

- Puree foods in a blender or food mill in quantity and freeze them in ice cube trays (or in "plops" on cookie sheets), then transfer to plastic bags. Cubes thaw quickly and are easy to take along for meals away from home.

- Feed a young child a banana right out of the peel, with a spoon, one bite at a time. The rest of the banana will stay fresh and not turn brown.

- Add a little liquid to soft-cooked meats to make them easier to grind in a baby grinder. In the same grinder, you can puree most of your own table foods, unseasoned, for your baby.

- Use a long-handled spoon that fits the baby's mouth. Plastic-coated spoons feel good on tender gums.

When There's No Highchair

"Trap" a small child for feeding (when a highchair's not available or the child is too small for one) and still provide comfort: cross your left leg over your right knee at the ankle, forming a triangle. (Reverse the position if you are left-handed.) Set the child in the triangle. He or she can't get out, can't squirm. A bonus is that you can feed the child between bites of your own meal.

- Keep the baby from sliding down in a highchair by putting a rubber sink mat or stick-on nonslip bathtub daisies or strips on the seat.

- Or use a commercially-made terrycloth highchair insert which helps a very young child sit up. The product is good for travel, too.

- Try using a molded plastic bib with a "lip"; it provides a good catchall. Or try to find a bib with cap sleeves to keep the baby's clothes clean. If the bib isn't waterproof on at least one side, save it for "drool and dribble."

- Sew scratchy vinyl bibs to the backs of terrycloth ones — soft under the baby's chin, but still waterproof.

- Tuck a double thickness of facial or toilet tissue under the neckline of the bib to keep drools from running down the baby's neck.

- Watch out — DUCK — if the baby sneezes with a mouthful of food!

Do-it-yourself eaters

Self-feeding is messy, and it often takes a child a long time to eat even a small meal, but you should encourage it anyway. Don't panic if your child prefers fingers to spoons; they're faster, and the feeling of food is as important to a child as its color and flavor. The finer points of etiquette can be picked up later. Just make things as easy as possible for the child (and yourself) and let him or her go to it!

- Put a rubber suction soap holder on the tray to keep the plate or bowl from slipping and to free both the baby's hands for eating.

- Pile the baby's food right on the highchair tray at first and avoid the problem of the thrown plate.

- Try a colorful bandana for a child who's a "bib-resister." The folds may catch some of the spills.

- Give a child who insists on eating from a big plate a plastic one with a raised rim. Some even have divided sections.

- Give the baby a spoon in each hand and use one yourself. The baby will imitate you. Demitasse or small sugar spoons and hors d'oeuvres forks (not too sharp!) are easy for babies to eat from. And for a real beginner, consider a wooden tongue depressor as a scoop for food.

- Give a butter spreader or plastic picnic knife to a child who wants all the tools for eating that grownups have.

Do-it-yourself drinkers

- Slip a bright-colored sock over the bottle to make it easier for the baby to hold.

- Let a toddler learn to drink from a cup in the bathtub.

- Or let the child drink from a plastic medicine or eyewash cup. They're easier to hold and won't soak him or her if they spill. A variation: three-ounce paper cups.

- Fill toddlers' glasses only about a third full to prevent waste if they're spilled.

- Draw or tape a circle on the highchair tray to show your child where the cup goes — not too close to the edge!

- Let your child use a bright-colored straw, or several of them, for drinking sometimes. Cut straws off two inches above the cup so the child won't tip the drink.

Easy eating

- Let a fussy child have a paper bag of small goodies while you prepare the meal — small edibles he or she can pull from the bag to feel and eat.

- Give your child cereal or soup in a cup or mug with a handle to grasp. Milk or broth remaining can be drunk instead of spooned out.

- Quickly cool food that's too hot for a toddler by dropping an ice cube into it.

- Fill the compartments of a muffin tin with different finger foods such as cheese cubes, strips of cold meat, crackers, raw vegetables or fruit. It's called a "potpourri lunch."

- Serve an occasional meal on a doll plate, an aluminum pie plate or a new Frisbee, just for fun.

- Mix yogurt or applesauce instead of milk with dry cereal for a manageable solid when a child hasn't yet mastered handling a spoon.

- Serve bran muffins slightly frozen — nutritious, and fewer crumbs.

- Use pureed meat or vegetables a baby won't eat as sandwich spreads; finger foods often go down more easily than those which must be eaten with a spoon.

- Or mash leftovers, mix them with an egg and cook like pancakes, or bake them in muffin tins.

- Fill an ice cream cone with tuna or egg salad, cottage cheese or yogurt for easy eating. It's a good on-the-run lunch for an older child, too.

- Let a preschooler make a "dangerous dinner." It's constructed with toothpicks held together with pieces of meat, chunks of cheese and vegetables, dried fruits — anything good. When it's "built," it's ready to eat.

- Teach even young children to get a cold meal for themselves — a sandwich or an already prepared salad from the refrigerator — so they can be self-sufficient sometimes.

Gnaw-ons for Teethers

- Frozen teething rings; chilled pacifiers.
- A chilled seedless orange, cut into sections. Or unpeeled chunks of apple or other fruits. (Beware of large chunks that a child with a few teeth might bite off and choke on.)
- A cold or frozen carrot or stringless cold celery. (Caution, as above.)
- A frozen banana, or a lengthwise-cut piece of one.
- The core of a fresh pineapple, cut into quarters. The core is not as strong-tasting as the rest of the fruit, but it still may be a bit too acid for some children.
- A cold or frozen bagel.
- A dampened washcloth or soft pot holder, frozen and stored in a plastic bag.
- An ice cube, tied into a washcloth with string.
- A toothbrush.
- Two or three very large jingle bells tied on a shoestring.
- A clean rubber canning ring.
- A new, clean rubber ring from the puppy department of your supermarket.
- Or a dog biscuit — really! They're not harmful in any way.

Cleanups: your child

- Take your child to the sink using the "football hold" (tucked under your arm) and make a game of washing hands and face after meals.

- Keep a step-stool handy for a child old enough to wash his or her own hands and face at the sink.

- Use your hand, dipped in water, to wash the face of a reluctant toddler. Most children don't seem to fight as much as if you use a cloth, and you'll do just as good a job.

- Let your child dip messy hands into a plastic bowl of water while still in the high chair. Then just wipe 'em dry.

- Squirt a little shaving cream on the child's cheeks and let him or her "shave" it off with a washcloth.

Cleanups: equipment

- Put a plastic tablecloth or a piece of oilcloth on the floor under the highchair, if you have kitchen carpeting, and wipe up spills easily. On a hard-surface floor, spread out a whole section of newspaper and pull off one page after each meal, wrapping the crumbs inside. Or get a non-finicky dog!

- Mount a regular lightweight paper towel holder, or one with suction cups, on the back of the highchair to hold towels for quick cleanups.

- Buy a highchair with a detachable tray, if you're getting a new one, for easiest quick cleanups.

- Rub waxed paper over the runners of a clean highchair to make the tray slide back on more easily. Or apply a bit of petroleum jelly or salad oil with a cotton ball.

- Put a plastic and metal highchair under the shower and let hot water spray over it for a few minutes. Caked-on food wipes off easily.

- Clean the highchair outdoors in the summer with the garden hose. Let it sit in the sun for a time to help disinfect it.

- Use a solution of water and dishwasher soap to loosen really crusty spills.

- Give your child an ice cream pail and a sponge and let him or her "help."

CLOTHING

As soon as possible, begin to give your child choices about clothes. Having a choice of three outfits can make all the difference with a finicky youngster and, for one who doesn't care, it provides practice in making decisions. Thereby begins the process of establishing a self-image.

When you select clothes for your child, you'll want to consider comfort, fit and durability. If you can't resist a ruffle, bow or bit of lace, make sure it's firmly attached (and wash the garment before it's worn, if the decoration is scratchy). Remember that knits are easier to care for than woven fabrics and more comfortable to wear. Front fasteners will be easier for your child (and for YOU, during that period when you must dress a child-in-motion). Necklines in slip-over clothing must be large enough to slip over the child's head without a struggle. Pre-schoolers need PLENTY of POCKETS for collecting things.

When you're the dresser

- Buy overalls with fasteners in the crotch for easy diaper changing.

- Distract a baby who's old enough to resist diapering by performing that task while he or she is standing up, perhaps watching television.

- Or talk to the child very rapidly, so that he or she will have to pay close attention to your face, not your hands.

- Give the child a toothbrush to manipulate or a toy to play with, or stick some masking tape on his or her fingers — it'll take a minute or two to get off.

- Or put up mirror tiles where a child can see himself or herself and share the tedium of diapering with a "friend."

- Dress a squirmy toddler on his or her tummy, if you can, for better control.

- Fasten overall straps in back with mitten clasps to keep them from sliding down a toddler's arm.

- Choose clothes with zippers rather than buttons to make dressing a wiggler easier.

- Run a bar of soap (the little ones from hotels are ideal) or a lead pencil over a sticking zipper.

- Put a small treat, such as a raisin or piece of dry cereal, into your child's hand so he or she will make a fist to push through a sleeve.

- Ask your child to make a fist when you're putting on mittens. When the mitten's on, ask the child to stick out the thumb first, then to open the fist.

- Attach mittens to a long string that goes through both coat sleeves if your toddler can undo mitten clips.

- Use knee-high socks as mittens — they can't be pulled off.

- Don't be surprised if the toddler you just dressed removes all his or her clothes within minutes. That's a skill to be mastered, too. (One-piece garments will help discourage undressing, if you really haven't time for it.)

Nighttime diapering

- Double diaper the baby, if you use cloth diapers, or put a sanitary pad (or part of one) inside a diaper.

- Use half of a cheap disposable, with tabs cut off and plastic perforated, as a liner for a better nighttime disposable.

- Slip one disposable into another that you've split at the top, with both plastic pieces at the outside.

- Use rubber or plastic pants over diapers, if your child doesn't have diaper rash problems.

Putting shoes on

- Put shoes on a squirmy toddler while the child is in the high chair. Or lightly tickle the bottom of the child's foot — toes will uncurl and shoes will go on smoothly.

- Wet shoelaces before tying them and as they shrink they'll tighten up and stay tied.

- Prevent the tongues of shoes from sliding out of place by cutting two small parallel slits in each tongue, a half-inch from the outside tip. Pull the laces through the slots and tie as usual.

- Put plastic bags over shoes before putting on boots, for ease of "entry." The bags will help keep shoes dry, too. They can be stapled into the boots if you like.

- Or spray the insides of boots with a dusting product containing wax and wipe until dry. The boots will slip on easily.

Daily use of footwear

- Stick T-shaped pieces of adhesive tape or nonslip bathtub appliqués on the bottoms of a baby's new hard-soled shoes to give more traction and help a young walker gain confidence. One package of appliques will last through several pairs of shoes, but if you don't want to make the investment, simply rough up the surface of the shoe sole with sandpaper.

- Cover shoes with large woolen socks to keep your child's feet extra warm and dry inside boots. Buy boots large enough to accommodate the extra layer.

- Repair rubber boots with materials from an inexpensive inner-tube repair kit, available at the hardware store.

- Use your portable hair dryer to dry winter boots quickly.

Save Time ... Save Pajamas

Have your kids dress at bedtime in clean clothes, if you can bring yourself to break old habits. Today's fabrics don't wrinkle, and the kids are ready to go in the morning.

Dressing themselves: closings

You'll want to encourage your child's every effort at self-dressing, even though it'll take a great deal more time at first and cause some frustration for both you and the child. If you can't resist helping, busy yourself elsewhere, close enough to be of assistance if needed, but giving the child a chance to handle it all alone.

- Make button-handling easier by sewing large buttons on your child's clothes and easier yet by sewing them on with elastic thread.

- Teach your child to button from the bottom up; chances of coming out even are better.

- Tie big wooden beads, buttons or small toys to the strings of hoods to keep the strings from being pulled out.

- Attach notebook rings to zippers on boots and jackets to make them more manageable. On boots, the rings can be hooked together for storage.

- Teach your child to pull a zipper AWAY FROM clothes and skin to keep it from catching.

Dressing themselves: other helps

- Buy pants and skirts with elasticized waistbands to make them easy to pull on and off, but be sure the elastic isn't so tight that it makes imprints on the skin or rides up.

- Mark the belt hole a child should use with a piece of masking or adhesive tape.

- Try to get clothing with monograms, appliques or other special trim on the front to help a child tell front from back. On homemade garments, mark an X in the back with colored thread.

- Teach your child to look for the label in the back of underpants. If there's no label, indicate the front by sewing on a "belly button" or drawing one with a marking pen.

- Sew loops of elastic thread inside the cuffs of sweaters and have your child loop them over his or her thumbs to hold sleeves down while putting on a coat or jacket.

- Help your child put on a jacket or coat: spread the garment on the floor, openings up, and have the child stand above it at the neck end, bend over, slip arms into sleeves and flip it over his or her head. Or have the child lie on his or her back on the garment, put arms in armholes and stand up.

XYZ!

You have a boy who's often caught with zipper down? Say "XYZ" to him —"Examine your zipper." Add "PDQ" — "Pretty darn quick!"

Helping with shoes

Shoes are not obligatory for new walkers — going barefoot gives little feet good exercise. For a child a little older, new shoes are often a great source of pleasure. They can also be a source of frustration. To help your child distinguish between the right and left shoes, mark the inside edges of both shoes with tape or a colored marker; when marks match, shoes are on the right feet. Or explain that if toes point "in," shoes "like each other" and are happy; going away from each other, they're sad.

- Coat the ends of shoelaces with clear nail polish or wrap them with masking tape when the plastic tips wear off.

- Tie knots at the ends of shoestrings after lacing them. The child can remove the shoes easily but won't pull the laces out.

- Avoid lacing and tying problems by substituting quarter-inch elastic for laces. Sew ends together at the top. The elastic stretches so that the shoe can be slipped on and off without untying.

- Keep shoelaces even at the ends by tying knots at their centers.

- Help a preschooler learn to tie shoes by letting him or her practice with one red and one black licorice string, which will let him or her see "which one is going over or under which." Success means, of course, that the child gets to eat the licorice.

Keeping clothes organized

- Hang coordinated sets of clothes in the closet or put complete outfits together in bureau drawers so that your child can select matching outfits.

- Organize socks for more than one child by assigning each a special pattern or color, or by buying a different brand for each.

- Buy all socks in the same brand and color for an only child to save the trouble of matching them.

- Pin pairs of tiny socks together with diaper pins for laundry and storage, and "pin" them to the clothesline.

- Use sew-on name tags for marking instead of iron-ons, which tend to wash out after three or four launderings.

- Or mark with an indelible pen, a liquid embroidery pen or an inexpensive rubber stamp that you can have made up at a stationery store.

- Write names on dark-colored boots and rubbers with a cotton swab dipped in bleach or with red marine paint, which holds up better than nail polish. If you prefer to mark inside the boots, use a marking pen.

Hand-me-downs

- Mark borrowed babies' or children's clothes that are to be returned so that you'll remember the lender. And label things YOU lend and want returned.

- Sort hand-me-downs according to season and size and label the boxes in which they're stored. Use disposable diaper boxes which designate weight or size to store appropriate baby clothes and small items. Really precious baby things — the ones you want to save forever — will be better preserved in self-lock plastic bags.

- Make boys' hand-me-downs feminine for girls by embroidering initials on pockets and designs around collars or cuffs and/or sewing on appliqués.

- Mark clothes with a single X or dot for the oldest child, two for the next, and so on. When clothes are handed down, it's easy to add another mark.

- Mark sizes on the inside waistbands of pants if labels have come off or become unreadable.

- Use the family last name only for marking outer clothes that you're sure will be handed down from one child to another.

- Avoid resentment over hand-me-downs by calling them "kindergarten dresses" or "first grade pants" instead of "Susie's" or "Jimmy's."

- Organize a neighborhood or church hand-me-down exchange. Pass around or leave in a centrally-located place a huge box of clothing from which each family takes out what's needed and puts in what's not.

Wise shopping for clothing

Some of the best-dressed children have the least amounts of money spent on their clothes. Garage sales, thrift shops, discount stores and manufacturers' outlet stores account for some savings (and thrift shops will take YOUR children's used clothing for sale on consignment). Hand-me-downs from relatives and friends also help. Clever shoppers try to keep a little cash on hand for an unexpected opportunity. Carrying a small notebook with measurements and sizes of all family members helps, too, and remember that for small children height and weight measurements are often more important than sizes. Remember to update your notebook often.

- Don't buy plastic pants with snaps; they rip off too easily.

- Buy "neutral" jeans, shirts and outer clothing so that they can be passed on to children of different sexes.

- Get "unisex" clothing in boys' departments; it's usually made more ruggedly and often costs less than that in girls' departments.

- Look for best quality in everyday wear such as underwear and in items which will be passed on to several children.

- Check for fit in socks if you aren't sure of size: have the child make a fist and wrap the sock around the fist over the knuckles. If the heel and toe meet, the sock will fit.

- Or buy tube socks. They wear evenly, are easy to put on and "grow" with kids.

- Buy shoes with laces for small children. Little slip-ons are cute and easy to put on, but they often don't STAY on.

- Try two-piece grow-a-size pajamas. If you always stick with the same color and brand, you can save good parts of outworn ones for patches.

- Or consider using bright T-shirts with iron-on transfers or embroidery for nightshirts.

- Buy smock-type dresses for girls; when they're too short they become tops to be worn over pants.

- Remember, when you buy snowsuits, that while one-piece garments are easier to put on, two-piece suits can be worn longer.

Home-sewn

"Get a good sewing machine and learn to use it, and learn to knit and crochet," is the advice of many parents who want their kids to be dressed well and economically. Work ahead of the seasons, they advise; think about hats and mittens and jackets in the summer, shorts and sun dresses after Christmas. Don't put hems in until it's time for kids to wear the garments.

When you select patterns and fabrics, try to imagine the finished product on your child. A style that suits the child's build and personality will look good and will contribute to his or her self-confidence. As the child grows, make notes on favorite patterns about larger waists and longer waists and arms. Remember that the fewer seams and built-in details, the easier the garment will be to make and the better it will look and wear. You can allow for growth by choosing styles with raglan or dolman sleeves and, in one-piece garments, with undefined waistlines. If you make double-breasted coats and jackets, you can realign buttons as the child grows.

- Wash (ALWAYS) all fabric before cutting to allow for shrinkage and for bleeding of colors. Use the water temperature and drying method you'll use for the finished garment.

- Sew on shank buttons and metal overall buttons with dental floss to keep them from being torn off.

- Put extra buttons on overall straps at longer lengths than a child needs. As he or she grows, the old ones can simply be snipped off. And sew double rows of snaps or buttons on two-piece sleepwear for the same reason.

- Apply clear nail polish over the tops of small buttons to help keep them from coming off and perhaps finding their way into a small child's mouth.

- Avoid sewing on buttons when you know you'll be moving them as a child grows. Sew thread through button eyes as if you're sewing the button onto cloth. Attach the buttons to the garment with safety pins run through the thread on the back . . . and repin as necessary.

- Sew an extra button or two to a piece of fabric from a garment and store it in your button box for easy finding at replacement time.

- Sew an extra button under the hem of a front-buttoning garment so that you'll have a matching one when the garment is lengthened.

- Use cellophane tape or masking tape when you're measuring and marking hems; it won't pinch or stab your child as pins will.

- Save handwork by using iron-on bonding materials for hems in lightweight fabrics.

- Put a long zipper from top to crotch in overalls for a boy who's toilet trained. A standard fly is usually hard to manipulate.

- Sew a sweater inside a coat as an extra liner.

- Make matching T-shirts (for siblings or for look-alike fun with friends or cousins) from one length of 60-inch-wide fabric.

- Use long dressmakers' pins with colorful plastic heads for sewing. They're easy to find and wonderful to sew with. Some mothers even count pins when sewing with small children around.

- Use empty vitamin bottles or other small containers with childproof caps to store pins and other little sewing notions. Contents are easily visible, yet safe from children.

Uses for Wonderful Velcro

- In small circles, in place of buttons, down the fronts of shirts and blouses and for waistband closures.

- Instead of buttons, to attach overall straps to overall bibs.

- Attached to mittens, to stick them together for storage.

- On overall straps in the back, to keep them from slipping down a child's arms.

- On washcloths, to make easy-to-change diapers for your child's baby doll.

- To make a "custom" T-shirt, attaching tiny stuffed animals or other little toys that your child can take on and off.

Making clothes last longer

- Fold two diapers together to fit an older baby, then stitch along each end to make "custom prefolds."

- Buy two-piece blanket sleepers for longer wear, and when they're too short extend their lives by cutting the feet off.

- Open the bottom seam on an outgrown one-piece blanket sleeper and use it for a beach cover-up.

- Turn nubby old tights inside out. They don't look much different, except that they're smooth again.

- Try tie-dying T-shirts that are badly stained.

- Reinforce the knees on new jeans (on the inside) with the extra fabric you trim from too-long legs or with iron-on patches.

- Cut too-short overalls apart at the waist and insert a wide band of matching or contrasting fabric.

- Lengthen girls' slacks by sewing on strips of grosgrain ribbon or decorative braid. Add similar trim or ruffles to the legs of pajama pants or cut off sleeves and legs to make summer pajamas.

- Lengthen suspender straps by sewing on extra fabric.

- Add another tier to tiered skirts or jumpers, using matching or contrasting fabric.

- Cut off floor-length dresses to make short ones for another year's wear.

- Cut the too-short sleeves out of an expensive quilted or padded jacket and let your child wear it as a vest over a heavy sweater.

- Extend the wear of jackets and snowsuits by sewing knitted cuffs (from the notions departments in fabric stores) to the ends of the sleeves.

Patching and covering up

- Patch the knees and feet of blanket sleepers with pieces of an old flannel-backed tablecloth.

- Cover old hemline marks on skirts or pants with zigzag stitching or sewn-on rickrack or ribbon bands.

- Run a dark blue crayon or indelible pencil over the white line on let-down jeans.

- Slip a rolled-up magazine into pants legs to avoid running through both thicknesses of material when pinning on patches.

- Or hold patches in place for stitching by gluing them on first. After sewing, wash the glue out.

- Cover a hole, mend or stain that shows by sewing on an appliqué.

Knit knacks

- Crochet mittens onto the sleeves of a sweater and they'll never get lost or separated.

- Wind leftover yarn from a knitted garment into a hank, tie it loosely and launder it with the garment. It will stay the same color as the garment and be ready for mending or lengthening.

- Unravel an outgrown sweater; wind the yarn loosely in hanks and tie in several places; wash. Rolled into balls, it's ready to reuse for a smaller child's garment.

- Use a pattern one size larger than your child needs when you knit or crochet a garment. If it takes a long time to finish, there's a better chance it will still fit.

- Use knitting and crocheting patterns that call for sport yarn or worsted weight instead of fingering yarn so your work will go faster.

Preventive maintenance

- Spray knees, cuffs and collars of garments with fabric protector (and the fronts of "best clothes" for a drooler or messy eater). Spills and such will bead up and dirt can be wiped off with a damp cloth.

- Sew squares of quilted material on the knees of pants for crawling babies; they protect both pants and knees.

- Put iron-on patches on the cotton soles of sleepers to keep them from wearing out.

Getting clothes clean

Today almost everything but the child goes into the washing machine. Bleach of one kind or another does wonders with really dirty clothes. Some parents change brands of laundry detergent occasionally, feeling that the new brand washes out the residue of the old, and clothes will be cleaner. If you take your laundry to a laundromat, carry your detergent in old baby food jars to lighten the load you must drag along.

And remember — there's NO LAW that says kids' play clothes must be spotless!

- Get grimy socks white by soaking them in a solution of washing soda and water before laundering. Or boil them in water with a sliced lemon.

- Dip a cotton swab in bleach and dab at stains on white bibs or clothes that have embroidery, appliqué or other unbleachable features.

- Sponge grass stains with alcohol (dilute with two parts water if fabric is acetate or noncolorfast) if regular laundering doesn't get them out. Or work liquid detergent or shampoo into the stain, rinse and launder as usual.

- Soak egg-stained clothing in cold water for an hour before laundering. Hot water will set the stain.

- Soak bloodstains in cold water for at least 30 minutes. If the stain doesn't come out, soak in an enzyme product or pour a few drops of ammonia on the spot. Or try using hydrogen peroxide before soaking in water.

- Soak vomit-stained clothes in cold water and sponge stains with a solution of a quart of ammonia and a half-teaspoon of liquid detergent.

- Remove food coloring stains from clothes by rubbing them with toothpaste. Let dry, rinse in cold water and launder as usual.

- Use a cup to a cup-and-a-half of vinegar in a gallon of water, or add a tablespoon of dishwasher crystals to a load of laundry for a bleach that's safe for nylon, rayon and all fine washables.

- Saturate tough stains, such as chocolate or grape juice, with club soda. Rub until discoloration is gone, then wash as usual.

- Use bottled rug shampoo with a brush (and lots of suds) for winter coats that need dry cleaning. It works on both wool and corduroy.

- Remove gum from clothing by softening it with egg white. Scrape it off and launder the garment as usual.

Caring for shoes

- Clean white baby shoes by rubbing them with a raw potato, liquid nonabrasive cleaner or alcohol before polishing. Or apply toothpaste with an old toothbrush, scrub gently and wipe off. Let dry before polishing.

- Spray newly polished white baby shoes with hair spray to prevent polish from coming off.

- Use pre-moistened towelettes to remove black marks from white shoes.

- Polish kids' shoes with an old nylon stocking for a high gloss. Or let polish dry thoroughly and buff with waxed paper.

- Clean sneakers with a soap-filled scouring pad. Use bleach or lemon juice in the rinse water if the shoes are white.

- Spray new sneakers with starch or fabric protector to keep dirt from becoming embedded.

SLEEPING

Getting children to sleep comfortably and fearlessly through the night is a problem most parents seem to have at various times. Just wait, though — teenagers usually sleep very well, and often late into the morning, when you'd like them to be up and about.

Determining bedtime

- Keep bedtime at the SAME time every night to help establish regular sleep habits.

- Relieve yourself of the onus of setting bedtime by letting the hands of the clock do the job.

- Set a timer to mark bedtime and let it go off early enough to give a little warning. Leftover time might be added to the bedtime ritual as a reward for hurrying.

- Have a "goodnight parade" if you have two or more children. The whole family marches through the house, stopping in the kitchen for water, in the bathroom for toothbrushing and toileting, in the living room (to lock the front door for the night). The "caboose" (youngest) is dropped off first.

- Or have your child put all toys to bed, one by one — and when they're all down, he or she is the LAST ONE to go to bed.

Helping children get to sleep

- Add a little cereal to the baby's bottle for the last feeding.

- Feed your older child a protein snack, if you offer a snack at all, before bedtime.

- Spend some quiet time before bedtime — **rough-and-tumble play excites a child.**

- Take a good long walk with your child before bedtime and follow it with a nice warm bath and some soothing music.

- Continue the sleep routine you probably started when your child was an infant.

- Put a few favorite dolls or stuffed animals in bed with your child and tell him or her the toys are ready to settle down. The child may cooperate by settling down himself or herself.

- Let even a little child "read" himself or herself to sleep — lying down — with a pleasant, non-scary book.

- Put soft stereo headphones on your child and let restful music induce sleep.

- Try using a tape recording on nights you can't read to your child at bedtime. It can be one you buy, with favorite songs and nursery rhymes, or one you tape yourself, with bedtime stories and lullabies.

- Give your child a relaxing mini-massage.

- Add interest to a child's backrub by "planting a garden," using different strokes for spading, raking, preparing the rows and planting the seeds of fruits and vegetables the child selects.

- Teach your child to relax every muscle, starting with the toes and moving up to the head. Eyes should be kept closed.

- Put a dab of cologne on the back of your child's hand and tell him or her to sniff until the scent is gone. Deep breathing and concentration usually bring sleep quickly.

- Have a nice snuggle with your child before sleep time, once he or she is in a big bed. It gives a parent a nice little rest and it's a warm tradition to start.

- Let your child pick from a "dream jar" (perhaps an empty can you've decorated) a slip of paper on which you've written an idea for a pleasant dream. The child can go to sleep with the paper beneath the pillow.

Night wakers

Some parents let a wakeful child cry after checking to make sure there's nothing really wrong, and they say the crying shortens in duration over a few nights and soon stops altogether. If you can't bear to do that, keep in mind the facts that often simply picking up and cuddling a child for a few minutes will do the trick and that night waking doesn't last forever. IGNORE the advice of well-meaning friends and relatives whose children "always slept all night."

- Give your child a bottle, if you wish, but if he or she has teeth, make it plain water only. Milk or any sweetened drink may lead to severe tooth decay.

- Keep several pacifiers in the crib, but NEVER tie one on a string around a baby's neck. It might get tangled and cause strangulation.

- Take the child back to bed with you. One "family bed" variation is a king-sized bed with a one-side-removed-crib pushed up against it. Another is a guard rail on one side of the bed; the parents needn't be separated with a child between them, yet there's no worry about the child falling out of bed. For some, family sleeping equals comfort. Those who like the idea (not everyone does!) say it fulfills a basic human need for warmth, closeness and security.

- Use an incentive chart for a child if you don't want company in your bed. Draw stars on a calendar with marking pens (let the child choose the color) for each night he or she doesn't come to your bed. Ten stars might earn a small present.

- Put a small mattress (or a big pillow) and a blanket on the floor near your bed for the nighttime waker who needs to fall back to sleep near you.

- Use a nightlight in the room if the child wants one, or let the child have a flashlight. Or try a lighted fish tank, which offers not only light, but movement as well.

- Have your doctor check for a physical reason for unusually frequent waking. The child may have a middle ear infection. The flat position of sleeping increases the pressure behind the eardrum and causes pain.

Sleepwalkers

- Guide a sleepwalker back to bed, awake or asleep (myths about it being bad to wake a sleepwalker are just that — myths), talking quietly and reassuringly. Stop at the bathroom before going back to the child's bedroom, then stay with the child until you are sure he or she is sleeping well again.

- Take precautions: block stairways with gates and put secure locks on doors that lead outside.

- Or put a gate across the child's doorway, or even a chain lock on the outside of the door. Either will allow you to peek inside, yet still keep the child from getting out.

- If sleepwalking is frequent, check with your doctor. There may be a physical reason for it.

Delaying the "early riser"

- Put a few cloth books or soft toys in a small child's crib for morning play. But do it after the child is asleep.

- Attach an unbreakable mirror to the inside of the crib so a baby or toddler can amuse himself or herself for a few extra minutes in the morning.

- Leave a "surprise bag" by the bed of an older child or fasten a bicycle basket or plastic pail to the side of the crib — also after the child is asleep. Put in any selection of small items for quiet play — books, games or things to create with, such as pipe cleaners, bits of fabric, crayons and paper.

- Add a bite to eat for a child who will be hungry and who can handle it. One good snack that consumes a great deal of time is raisins, wound every few inches into a strip of waxed paper formed into a "snake." (Some don't put food out, though, feeling that it may attract undesirable animals or insects.)

- Set an alarm clock or clock radio for one who ALWAYS wakes early. When it goes off, he or she may get up. Or set up two clocks for a preschooler, one running, the other unwound and set at getting-up time. When the hands of the second match those of the first, the child may get up.

Naps

- Try "white noise" in a little one's room if older non-nappers' playing keeps him or her from sleeping. Set up a small fan on a high dresser, directing the flow of air away from the child, and let it hum away.

- Make a naptime nook for a toddler in a large cardboard box decorated with bright drawings or decals inside and padded comfortably.

- Let your child nap in a sleeping bag on YOUR bed, the family room couch or the floor of his or her own room, just for variety.

- Call naptime by another name such as "rest time" or "quiet time" for a child who resists sleeping. Sometimes the child will actually fall asleep, but even if he or she doesn't, the time alone will be relaxing.

- Set an alarm clock or timer for a resting child, or put on a few long-playing records, to mark the end of rest time.

Going Visiting

The friend you're visiting doesn't have a crib — and your infant needs a nap? Settle the baby down in the bathtub with a big cushion or a few soft towels for a mattress! Be sure to remove soap and other bathing equipment!

Chapter 3

Hygiene and Health

Parents of young children usually spend a good deal of time in the bathroom...but not by themselves! Trying to keep active kids clean, introducing them to the art of cleaning themselves and getting them to use the toilet are time-consuming operations. Here are some ideas to make that time pay off.

SOAP AND WATER

When there are two or more little bodies to be bathed (or even just one), many parents find the assembly line method fast and easy. One parent washes and shampoos, the other dries and assists with pajamas.

Bathing and shampooing

- Use a clean plastic syrup bottle or dishwashing detergent bottle as a baby shampoo dispenser. The pull-up top lets you squirt just the right amount and reclose it with one hand.

- Take your child into the shower with you to help accustom him or her to water on the head and face.

- Strap a baby into an infant seat, with a towel replacing the pad, if you use a big tub for a baby who can't sit alone.

- Let a toddler play in a small, open mesh plastic laundry basket in the big tub as a transition from the baby bathtub. The basket can serve as a place to store the bath toys when the bath is finished.

- Or try using a plastic inflatable pool in the shower stall, also as a transition.

Play in the bath

- Keep bath toys in a nylon net bag and hang it from a faucet or shower head to drip dry.

- Make inexpensive, super bath toys by cutting colored sponges into interesting shapes.

- Let bath time be "science time" — provide a variety of things that sink and float; plastic glasses tall and thin, short and fat; large and small cups for measuring and pouring.

- If your toddler hates to leave the tub, pull the plug. When there's no more water for play, he or she will probably leave willingly. Or set a timer to go off when playtime is over.

- Or make two simple rules: "You're through when you stand up" or "You're through when your skin is wrinkled and you look like a raisin."

- Use the time while your toddler is playing in the tub to clean the rest of the bathroom.

Caution!
**Never leave a small child unattended in a bathtub —
even if an older sibling's present!**

Fear of the bath water

- Bathe with your child to provide extra security... and besides, it's fun!

- Run the bath water before bringing a frightened child into the bathoom, if you don't have another child who might climb in while your back is turned.

- Ask your child to help you put in a nonskid mat, lots of toys and bubble bath, for diversions. Some parents prefer to use a little liquid dishwashing detergent for bubbles. Bubble bath has been known to contribute to vaginal infection in little girls.

- Use only a few inches of water in the tub, increasing the amount as your child begins to get more comfortable with the water.

- Drain the tub after the child is out. Some are afraid that they, too, may go "down the drain."

Scared of shampooing

Most first-time parents are surprised when this fear develops, yet it's common. Shampoo as seldom as possible during this period — once or twice a week is probably often enough, unless there are special problems. Instead, brush hair frequently, give dry shampoos with a hairbrush covered with an old nylon stocking and occasionally "wash" hair with a damp washcloth. When you must shampoo, use a no-sting baby shampoo and do the job quickly and matter-of-factly, praising your child for "bravery." As difficult as this period is for you both, remember that it WILL pass.

- Shampoo your child first and then let him or her play so the bath will end on a happy note.

- Put a little lather on the child's hand and let him or her shampoo a doll while you shampoo the child.

- Make soap sculptures in the hair with shampoo and keep a hand mirror handy so that the child can admire them and watch the whole process.

- Try reintroducing a no-longer-used infant seat; the tilt allows the child's head to be tipped back comfortably for shampooing.

- Tell your child the story of a speck of dirt that gets tired, settles for a nap on the child's head and is joined by lots more specks, only to get washed out by Mom or Dad. The ritual of the story should last as long as the shampoo does.

- Or sing loud songs together throughout the whole shampoo process.

- Wrap the child in a big beach towel and lay him or her on the kitchen counter, face up, with head over the sink. Use a sink spray, if one's available. The towel holds the child steady, it is easier for you to control the soap and water, and your closeness gives security.

- Put only a small amount of water in the tub so the child can lie down flat for shampooing.

- Fill a big plastic jug with water and let it sink to the bottom of the tub — the child can use it for a headrest.

- Have the child lean back under the faucet for a quick, easy rinse. Or make things fun by using his or her own little watering can for the rinse.

- Use a sponge instead of a cup to control water when you rinse. (And try a sponge for applying shampoo — soap won't be so likely to run into eyes.)

- Give your child a small folded towel or washcloth to hold over his or her face. Or use a shampoo hat or swimming goggles.

To Remove Gum from Hair
Use peanut butter. Work it into hair, comb out gum and peanut butter. Shampoo. Cold cream also works, as do olive oil and witch hazel. (And try baby oil to remove gum from skin, or press a second wad of gum over the first and lift both off together.)

CLEAN AND NEAT

With babies and toddlers, the "finer points" of grooming are your responsibility and you don't want to encourage self-help with such tools as scissors and cotton swabs. As children grow, they often begin to take pleasure in looking nice and smelling good. If they start out with serviceable habits, they'll be apt to stick with them.

Encouraging good habits

- Keep a sturdy stepstool next to the sink to encourage self-help.

- Hang a small medicine cabinet on the bathroom wall at child's eye level to hold grooming necessities. If the small cabinet is mirrored, so much the better.

- Or buy mirror tiles you can stick on the wall at child height so your child won't have to climb. If possible, position the tiles where you can add additional ones above them as the child grows.

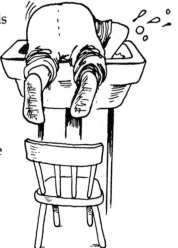

- Give your child a personal hygiene kit, an inexpensive plastic carrying case with his or her name on it. Equip it with a travel-size tube of toothpaste, a toothbrush, a small cake of soap and other necessities.

- A liquid soap dispenser is probably NOT a good idea until children are about five and will not use it as a plaything.

Using hand towels

The best way to get really dirty hands clean is to have a child wash something in the sink — a toy, a doll, some plastic cups. Remember that you really like a wet, dirty towel better than a neatly hung, unused one.

- Consider assigning each member of the family towels of different colors.

- Or buy washcloths and hand towels printed with pictures of favorite storybook characters for the kids.

- Place press-on hooks at your child's level so that towels can be hung up more easily.

- Attach a hand towel to a towel bar with a shower curtain hook or blanket clip. It will hang securely for hand drying.

- Give a bath mitt to a child who hates to wash up. Make it out of an old sock tied up with soap inside, or sew two washcloths together and put soap chips inside.

Cutting nails

- Cut an infant's nails at nursing time, with his or her head propped on a pillow so that you have both hands free.

- Cut nails while the infant or child is asleep.

- Use round-ended scissors, for safety's sake. Or try a nail clipper; some say it's easier to use than scissors. (Try keeping one on your key ring for quick clips when the baby sleeps while you're away from home.)

- Put talcum powder in your palm and scrape your child's nails over it. Enough will stick under the nails to show you how far to cut without causing hurt.

- Put a squirmy toddler in the highchair and give him or her something to eat. Or cut nails right after a meal, when the child is sleepy and content.

- Let your child watch television, as a distraction, while you cut his or her nails.

- Or try filing a child's nails.

- When nail-cutting is finished, clean under little nails with a flat wooden toothpick.

Cutting hair

Keep in mind that time is of the essence when cutting hair. Use sharp shears. What can't be done in five minutes probably won't get done. Try to insist that haircutting is a job for adults ONLY. If your preschooler abides by this rule, you'll be lucky!

- Cut a baby's hair while he or she sleeps. Results may not be high style, but the bulk of it will be off without a scene.

- Call a haircut a "trim." CUTS hurt!

- Set a child in a highchair or on a high stool for the job — outdoors in the summer. Spread newspaper to catch falling hair, even outdoors, because hair doesn't disintegrate as yard clippings do.

- Wrap a child in a large beach towel or small sheet when cutting hair to keep falling hair from slipping into the neck and becoming itchy.

- Put a piece of transparent tape (or special hair tape, which pulls off easily) across bangs and cut evenly above it.

- Try placing a piece of cardboard or paper between the child's hair and forehead when cutting hair to keep hair snips and the cold scissors away from the face.

- Or let the child wear a Halloween mask, which will keep hair from eyes. Be sure to have a mirror handy so the child can admire the effect.

- Try cutting hair with electric hair clippers (they tickle!). If Mom cuts Dad's hair with them too, it helps kids to see that HE isn't scared. And if a child is good, end the haircut on a high note with a few drops of men's cologne.

- When home haircutting becomes a struggle (between parent and child or parent and parent) it's time to change tactics and take your child to a barber. Consider going to one who specializes in cutting children's hair, at least for the first time or two, to set a pleasant tone for future haircuts.

- Prepare a child for a first professional haircut by letting him or her watch you or a sibling have a haircut.

DENTAL CARE

Diet is the first line of defense for good dental care; between-meal snacks and highly sugared foods contribute to decay. Frequent brushings remove the plaque that leads to decay. Brushing after snacks, even healthful ones like raisins or fruit juice, is particularly important. Toddlers and preschoolers, however enthusiastic, need help with toothbrushing; the manual dexterity necessary to thoroughly clean every surface of every tooth doesn't develop until the age of six or seven. To show your child where plaque collects on teeth and where decay can start, use a disclosing solution that you buy at the drugstore.

Your child's routine dental exams should begin, dentists recommend, when two or three teeth are in. Some parents take their children to their regular family dentists; others prefer pedodontists, who are specially trained to deal with the anxieties and emotions of youngsters. It is as important for a dentist to watch the shape of a child's mouth — to check the child's bite — as to check for cavities.

Toothbrushing routines

- Consider cleaning your infant's first tooth or two with a small gauze pad, with or without toothpaste. Rub the pad over the teeth and gums very gently to remove plaque and food debris. You'll probably find it easier to do this with the child's head on your lap.

- Let your child use an electric toothbrush if he or she likes the vibration. The cordless kinds are the easiest to handle. At least let him or her use the little brush — it's small enough to fit a tiny mouth.

- Offer a selection of toothbrushes, in all colors, and one or more toothpastes that the child likes. The small samples or travel sizes are favorites. (You may find that mint flavored toothpastes are too strong for your child's sensitive taste buds.)

- Try using an egg timer, with the rule that brushing continues until the sand is down. Or use a kitchen timer set for a specific length of time, or, for a change, a music box or a record.

- Let the child brush in the tub sometimes, where he or she can splatter, drool and gargle to heart's content.

- Let your child perform toothbrushing routines with you, both for the company and so you can set an example. Some children are even allowed to brush their parents' teeth so they can perfect their techniques.

- Hang a small mirror at the child's eye level so he or she can watch the action.

- Get across EARLY the idea that the tooth fairy pays a whole lot more for a perfect tooth than for a decayed one. In some families, the tooth fairy leaves with the "payment" a note praising the child for good dental habits.

TOILET TRAINING

While you may wish to choose the time to toilet train your child (obviously, spring and summer are the most convenient seasons), be aware that no child will be trained until he or she is ready — perhaps at 24 to 27 months or even older. Some of the signs of readiness are dry diapers for a couple of hours at a time; ability to understand simple commands and explanations and to mimic adults at other bathroom routines, such as brushing teeth or washing hands; an inclination toward tidiness, such as lining up shoes or toys neatly; and a dislike of being wet or soiled.

Remember that if you try to push things you'll only be training yourself. Put the whole thing off for a few weeks or months if it doesn't seem to be "taking." Relax, and don't pay too much attention to friends' and relatives' advice. By the time your child goes to school, you'll wonder why toilet training seemed such a big deal.

Basic training

Help your child understand, once "basic training" is under-way, that toilet habits are his or her own, including cleanups after accidents. Make it clear that this is not a punishment — just a matter of taking care of oneself.

- Put the potty chair in the bathroom some months before you think your child will be ready to use it. Explain that when he or she is old enough, it will be there to use.

- Try letting your child go without bottom clothing altogether, when training starts, to make things easier for you both. (You'll have to be a little brave to do this, or at least be a really good observer!)

- Make potty chair cleaning easier for yourself right from the beginning by putting an inch or so of water in the bottom of the pot.

- Let your child learn by watching you or an older child. (If the potty chair is set up near the big toilet, you can "go" together.) Imitation seems to be especially attractive to boys.

- Buy oversized, inexpensive training pants to make pulling up and down easy. They sometimes shrink as much as two or three sizes after laundering. The extra absorbency of expensive pants won't prevent them from becoming soaked if you're not using rubber pants over them.

- Put a potty chair on the floor in the back of the car, when traveling, so you can stop along the road instead of having to worry about finding a gas station in a hurry. A little boy can do nicely with an empty coffee can.

- Consider using an incentive chart, with stars or other stickers to mark days or parts of days without accidents, as you may do for other accomplishments. Some parents keep a supply of small toys in a big glass bowl, where they can be easily seen, to use as daily rewards for successful toileting.

- Turn on the faucet and let the water run for a few minutes; sometimes the sound of running water will bring "inspiration."

Using the big toilet

Some children are afraid of the big toilet. Explaining the body waste process and showing the child the sewer pipes and other plumbing may help overcome fears.

- Let a child who has a potty chair use the big toilet occasionally so he or she can use one comfortably away from home.

- Teach a little girl to sit backwards on the big toilet (some boys even like this position) or to perch on it sideways. And supply a step stool to help her climb up and down.

- Give a little boy a stool to stand on in front of the toilet. Be specific in teaching him to aim before starting to urinate, perhaps by floating a piece of tissue in the toilet as a target.

- If a step stool isn't available, let a boy kneel backwards on the seat, facing the back of the toilet.

Bedwetting

Nighttime wetting, which can continue into the preschool years (and beyond, more often for boys than for girls), is frustrating for child and parent alike. It's wise to check with your doctor to be sure there are no underlying physical causes for it. A recent report indicates that bedwetting for some children may be related to an allergic response to cows' milk. For others, it's simply that they're at an age of very sound sleep, during which a child doesn't "read" the body's signals. In this case, it's usually just a matter of waiting it out. It's really the child's problem, parents should remember — but there are a few ways to make things easier.

- Protect the child's mattress and, if necessary, the pillow too, with a zippered plastic cover. Or use a mattress pad with the plastic side down. Place a large towel between the pad and the sheet and you'll need only to change and wash the towel. Or slip the old waterproof sheet from the crib or an old plastic tablecloth between the bottom sheet and the mattress pad.

- Consider making up the child's bed with two sets of bedding, including two rubber sheets, so you need only remove one set for a dry bed in the middle of the night.

- Try getting the child up in the night for a trip to the toilet before you retire. This won't CURE bedwetting, but it may save a WET BED.

- Restrict fluids during the late afternoon and evening hours before bedtime.

- Help your child increase bladder capacity by having him or her wait as long as possible before urinating during the day.

- If you use diapers at night, double-diaper your child. For a larger child, you can buy adult-sized diapers from a hospital supply company.

- Help your child imagine, at bedtime, the possibility of a whole DRY night — the power of positive thinking! You might wish to add the use of an incentive chart to turn thinking into visible progress.

- Assure your child that bedwetting for which there is no physical cause WILL BE outgrown, EVENTUALLY.

FIRST AID

The most carefully reared and watched child will sometimes be hurt...or uncomfortable...or sick. Knowing ahead of time what to do for minor things that don't require a doctor's immediate attention gives parents a sense of control that's comforting. A good first-aid booklet and a book or two on home medical care are recommended. (The first-aid booklet belongs in the bathroom, where you may want it in a hurry. Protect its cover with clear contact paper.)

Remaining calm yourself will help calm your child in a crisis. Remember that a good venting cry may be the best thing for a hurt child, female OR male. When you think your child has cried long enough, tell him or her so. The idea is to teach the child that feelings should be expressed, but that there's also a time to regain control.

Handling ouches

- Make pain time applause time. The whole family can gather to praise bravery under difficult conditions.

- Use a red or other dark-colored washcloth to clean a bloody wound; the blood won't show, and the child will be less scared. Likewise, keep red paper napkins on hand to blot blood before you wash.

- Pin an "ouch" sign on clothes over a sensitive scraped area or injection to alert playmates to be careful. (But be aware that kids older than four or five may find it fun to HIT, right THERE!)

- Paint a funny face or animal with Merthiolate on a small sore area.

- Help a child stop crying by asking him or her to whistle. It's impossible to cry and whistle at the same time.

- Supply a "pain bell" for a child to ring or a whistle for him or her to blow until treatment has been completed.

- Have a child count while a shot or injection is being given to "see how long it takes," just for distraction.

- Coach your child in the relaxing and breathing techniques of prepared childbirth methods to lessen pain. Breathe in time together!

Bumps and bruises

Heat or cold . . . which should you use to keep swelling down and speed healing? Cold will help stop the bleeding under the skin that causes black and blue marks — but use it for only 24 hours after a bruise occurs. After that, heat, applied five or six times a day for the next few days, will speed recovery. Moderation is the key word — nothing TOO hot or TOO cold. Don't apply ice cubes directly to tender skin (wrap them in a washcloth) and don't use a high setting on a heating pad.

- Keep a supply of ice popsicles in the freezer for pleasurable treatment of a bumped lip.

- Try putting the inside of a piece of banana skin on a bruise and cover it with a cool, wet cloth to prevent excessive discoloration. (Particularly good for a black eye — and far less expensive than the traditional beefsteak!)

- Freeze wet washcloths or water in zip-lock freezer bags to apply to lumps, bumps or minor burns.

- Or freeze uncooked rice in a tightly closed plastic bag for a flexible compress.

- Use a can of frozen juice concentrate as a quick, non-drip frozen compress.

Bandaging

Probably no item in your medicine chest is as "magical" in its healing properties as a single adhesive bandage. And if one is good, several are even better. Plain ones, colored ones or those YOU decorate with self-adhesive colored dots all work wonders!

- Let your child put an adhesive bandage on the same ouch-spot on a doll so that pain can be shared and thus lessened.

- Cover a chafed or scraped knee or elbow with the cutoff top of an old sock to give extra protection to the bandage underneath and yet allow for active movement. A variation of this protection is a terrycloth tennis wristband.

- Make a popsicle stick splint for an injured finger or slip a small plastic hair roller over the bad finger to protect it from painful knocks.

- Put medicine on the bandage — not the sore — when it is necessary to apply something that stings.

- Saturate a piece of cotton with baby oil and rub it over the adhesive part of the bandage for easy removal.

Splinters

- Get your supplies arranged before you start: a bright light, perhaps a magnifying glass, and tweezers or a sterile needle. (You can sterilize a needle by holding it in a flame for a few seconds.)

- Prepare the splinter area by soaking it in warm water or olive oil, or covering it with a wet bandage or a piece of adhesive tape for a few hours, or holding the area over steam (from the mouth of a small bottle of boiling water). Any of these will loosen the splinter.

- Paint hard-to-find splinters with Merthiolate or iodine; they'll show up as dark slivers.

- Numb the splinter area with ice or a little teething lotion.

- Ask your child to look the other way and sing a song, count or recite something while you prod gently at the splinter with the sterile needle.

- If you can't get a splinter out, let well enough alone. Most splinters eventually work themselves to the surface. (For one that just doesn't, you may want to see your doctor.)

Treating bites and stings

In addition to the host of commercial products available, many simple household remedies work well.

- Rub a bar of wet soap over the bite, or apply toothpaste to it.

- Apply a paste of water and meat tenderizer. A paste of baking soda and water applied IMMEDIATELY to a bee or wasp sting reduces pain and swelling.

- Cut off the tip of an aloe plant and apply the sap to the bite, or buy aloe gel at a health food store. (It's also good for sunburn.)

- Hold ice, or ice wrapped in a cloth, on the sting area until it's numbed.

- Crisscross the swollen area around a mosquito bite with a fingernail (on the theory that one pain will cancel another) and apply some ever-available spit.

- Let an itchy child soak in a tub of water to which baking soda or laundry starch has been added. Or go to the beach, just for the sake of getting into the soothing water!

Child Has a Bug in the Ear?

First try taking the child into a dark room and shining a flashlight just outside his or her ear. Insects are often attracted by the light and just crawl out. If that doesn't work, drip a few drops of rubbing alcohol into the ear to kill the bug, then have the child turn his or her ear down and the bug will probably drop out. Never try to get hold of a bug with tweezers or other instruments; you're apt to push the bug farther in and there's a chance you could rupture the child's ear drum.

IN SICKNESS AND IN HEALTH

We experienced our parents' care when we were sick as children ... but the job of caring for our own sick children seems awesome. As parents we act as paramedics, comforters and companions to our sick children. Until your children can TELL you what is bothering them, these roles can be especially difficult to play.

Many of the ideas in the section YOUR BABY'S DOCTOR apply to the care of toddlers and preschoolers as well as infants.

Taking temperatures

The rectal temperature is the most accurate. It will be one degree higher than an oral temperature. Other methods are possible for "ball park" temperatures when you simply want an indication as to whether a child is running a fever.

One way is to kiss your child's forehead (the temperature of your lips is more stable than that of your hands). The axillary (armpit) method is used by some parents, the commercially available forehead strip by others. It's important to tell your doctor which method you have used when you report a temperature.

- Make insertion of a rectal thermometer easier by smearing petroleum jelly on it.

- Give a child an egg timer or kitchen timer to watch while his or her temperature is being taken.

- Or let the child watch TV or listen to a record to shorten the wait.

Giving medication

One of the hardest things about giving medicine to babies and small children is getting it ALL DOWN. Don't try putting it in a bottle of formula or juice; you won't know how much the baby has received if all the liquid is not taken.

- Give a baby liquid medicine in a nipple. (Flush the nipple with a little water for the child to suck, to be sure all medication is taken.) Or use an eyedropper or vitamin dropper, or a disposable 5 cc syringe (without the needle), which you can buy at the drugstore. Squirting is easy, there's no mess, and 5 cc's equal one teaspoon.

- Get a hollow, graduated medicine spoon from your druggist for dosing older children.

- Hold a paper cup under a child's chin when giving liquid medicine. Spills can be mixed with water or fruit juice and drunk from the cup.

- Butter a pill lightly or coat it with salad oil and it will go down easily. Or bury it in a spoonful of applesauce.

- Or press the pill between two spoons to crush it, then mix it with applesauce or jam. Serve it by spoon with a "chaser" of water or juice.

- Taste medicine yourself, and tell your child if it will taste bad. And if it will, rub an ice cube over the child's tastebuds on the tongue to kill the taste.

- If a child absolutely refuses medicine, with clamped jaws, gently squeeze his or her nostrils shut. The mouth will open quickly!

Constipation

Children are as variable in bowel movement patterns as they are in height and weight. Constipation is best treated by diet: encourage a child to drink lots of water and fruit juice (especially prune juice); give him or her high-fiber foods, such as bran cereal; give dried fruits as snacks. For an infant, add a teaspoonful of dark corn syrup to an eight-ounce bottle of formula or milk. A doctor should be consulted if a child has great pain in passing stools or if blood appears in stools. Parents whose children sometimes have just a little difficulty have thought up ways to help.

- Spread a little petroleum jelly on the child's rectum or on a thermometer which you insert in the child's rectum, as you would to take a temperature.

- Sit in the bathroom with your child. Little bottoms don't fit comfortably on adult toilet seats and moral and physical support helps.

- Help your child hold the "cheeks" open to make passage easier.

- Ask your doctor for a relaxant medicine if you feel your child has an especially "tight" rectum.

Diarrhea

Diarrhea can be caused by a number of serious illnesses or allergies; if it continues for several days, your doctor should be consulted. Most often, though, it's just a nuisance and a mess. One worry connected with long-lasting diarrhea is dehydration, for which a doctor should definitely be called. If your child is listless and lethargic and refuses liquids, suspect dehydration. Other symptoms are inability to retain liquids consumed, infrequent urination, dry mouth, few tears when the child cries, fever and dry skin. One test for dehydration is to pinch up a small fold of skin on the back of a child's hand. If it fails to sink back down when released, dehydration may be present.

- Encourage the child with diarrhea to drink lots of clear liquids, including broth and carbonated drinks (let them stand for a few minutes or stir to remove bubbles), sugar water or Gatorade, but NOT milk. Give ONLY liquids during severe diarrhea.

- Or give Jell-O water. This homemade "binder" is made by dissolving a three-ounce package of Jell-O in a cup of cold tap water.

- Or try water in which rice has been cooked; it's a "binder," too.

- Don't give a commercial "binding" product to a child under five or six without consulting your doctor.

Calling the Doctor

Try not to have to hold a crying baby while you call the doctor; neither you nor the doctor will be able to hear very well.

The heave-ho's

- Give ice chips instead of water to a child who can't keep liquids down. A child shouldn't drink after vomiting, but ice chips will help remove the bad taste.

- Place a plastic wastebasket on the floor next to the bed of a child who has been vomiting. An additional precaution is to have a plastic mixing bowl and bath towel by the child's side.

- Or spread towels over the child's pillow and blanket; they are easier to remove and launder than bed linens.

Colds and flu

- Use a soft old terrycloth baby washcloth or a man's large, soft handkerchief instead of a tissue to wipe a tender nose.

- Use an electric coffee maker with the lid off if a steamer or vaporizer isn't available when you need one. Be sure to place it where it can't be tipped over.

- Or let very hot water run in the shower or tub and sit in the bathroom with the child, with the door closed.

- Hang a wet towel or sheet near a heat source to increase the humidity in a room and make labored breathing easier.

- Put a feverish child in a lukewarm tub and let him or her blow bubbles. When the child is bored with that activity, give him or her a popsicle to eat in the tub — fun, no mess, and the fever comes down.

Coughs and sore throats

- Elevate the head of the mattress to ease breathing for a child with croup or a bad cough by placing a folded blanket underneath it. Or raise the head of the bed with a few books under the bed legs.

- Make a cough medicine by mixing lemon juice and honey in equal parts. (Do not give honey to babies under one year old; there is some concern about its safety for infants.)

- Teach a child to gargle by doing it yourself while singing a song, letting the child join in.

- Let very hot water run in the shower or tub and sit in the bathroom with the child, with the door closed, for the heavy steam that helps croup.

Ear infections

- Eliminate or cut down the child's intake of dairy products to help reduce the mucus that contributes to ear infection.

- Elevate the head of the mattress to help fluid drain.

- If you worry about using a big ear dropper for oil your doctor prescribes, try warming the oil in the small glass vial from a home pregnancy test kit and applying it with the small dropper from the kit. If you can do it while the child is asleep, so much the better.

Sickroom logistics

- Keep medications, paper cups and other sickroom supplies in a container such as a shoe box or bread pan to save running from room to room.

- Or use a lazy susan for easy access to bedside supplies.

- Anchor a shoe bag between bed mattress and foundation. The pockets, hanging down over the edge, will hold tissues and other small necessities.

- Pin a paper bag to the side of the mattress for soiled tissues and other scraps.

- Keep a bell or whistle near a child's bed so he or she can summon help when it's needed. (But tell the child to ring or blow just once or twice — not continually!)

- Be aware that your child may sometimes ask for a drink just to have your attention, but if it doesn't happen too often, go along with it.

- Make a table over a child's bed by using an adjustable ironing board, a card table with two legs folded up or a big cardboard box cut out to fit over the child's legs.

- Let a sick child lie on an adjustable chaise lounge from your outdoor furniture set. It allows for a variety of positions and saves continual propping.

- Use a parent's old T-shirt as a sick gown for a child with chicken pox, a rash, poison ivy or any eruptions that require lotion. The shirt won't bind and the lotion won't stain bedding or furniture.

- Serve tray meals with a damp washcloth or paper towel under the dishes to prevent them from slipping. The towel can be used to clean the patient's hands after eating.

- Cover the top blanket with a sheet that can be changed if food or liquid is spilled on it.

Casts on arms and legs

- Keep a plaster leg or arm cast dry for showering or bathing by covering it with a large plastic bag held in place with waterproof electrical or plastic tape.

- Lubricate the edges of a cast with petroleum jelly to prevent chafed skin.

- Sprinkle baby powder at the opening of a cast and blow it in with a hair dryer or vacuum cleaner (with airflow reversed) to relieve itching.

- Clean a dirty cast, if you must clean it, with white shoe polish.

- Make regular jeans and pants usable over a leg cast by inserting a long zipper in the inseam. When the cast comes off, the zipper can be removed and the seam sewn up.

- Use a solution of three tablespoons of vinegar to a quart of warm water to soak off casts (such as those for children who "toe-in") that must be changed regularly. After soaking, use bandage scissors to begin unraveling the gauze.

Chapter 4

Coping with Kids at Home

The better organized a household is, the more smoothly it usually runs, but with children around, there's plenty of just plain COPING with one situation at a time. Nevertheless, there are things you can do to cope better!

CHILDPROOFING YOUR HOME

Obviously, there's no way to childproof a house 100 percent, but, for starters, get down on the floor on your hands and knees. Crawl through the route your child uses (or will use — you'll want to childproof BEFORE he or she starts moving); grab and pull on everything within your reach.

You'll discover objects just right to swallow, sharp edges on the undersides of furniture and loads of things that will break off or fall over. Remember, too, that childproofing (and child-watching!) when you're visiting will be YOUR responsibility.

The kitchen stove

- Turn all saucepan handles to the rear of the stove.

- Turn on the oven light when the oven's in use and teach children that "light on means hands off." Leave the light on until the oven is cool.

- Remove stove knobs, if you can, or tape them so they can't be turned on by children.

- Back a chair up to the stove for a young cook's helper and let him or her stand or kneel on it. The chair back provides a "barrier." (You're RIGHT THERE, of course.)

- Let children stir food on the stove with long-handled wooden spoons; wood doesn't transmit heat.

- Always set a timer when you're cooking with kids around. Children are distracting, and you can easily forget and cause a fire or ruin food.

Around the kitchen

- Tuck cords safely behind kitchen appliances so kids can't pull the appliances down on themselves.

- Use safety locks on drawers and cupboards. Several brands are available in hardware stores. Or you can run a yardstick through some kinds of drawer and cabinet handles or use metal shower rings or blanket clips, at least for a few months.

- Use wet paper toweling or paper napkins to pick up small pieces of broken glass the broom doesn't get so young crawlers won't cut hands and knees.

- Let children use plastic or paper cups instead of breakable glasses and china mugs.

- Store plastic cups in a drawer rather than in a cupboard. For the child who's able to reach the faucet with a stool, they'll be easier to get at.

- Move all cleaning supplies from that accessible space under the sink (store plastic containers and pans the kids can play with there instead) and LOCK THEM UP. If you don't use Mr. Yuk stickers, paint the caps of dangerous materials with red nail polish and teach children that RED means DANGER.

- Beware of a child tasting detergent from the soap cup in the dishwasher; add it only when you're ready to start the machine.

- Prevent smashed toes by keeping shoes on a child who will be pulling cans or heavy objects from a kitchen cupboard.

- Don't use tablecloths until your child in the highchair is past the grabbing stage.

- Make loops of strong shoelaces and attach them to the back rounds of the highchair (and also the stroller and car seat) and run a belt through them to keep your child from climbing out.

The bathroom

The potential for poisoning in the bathroom is perhaps even greater than in the kitchen. A locking medicine chest is well worth the inconvenience it causes adults, and Mr. Yuk stickers give additional protective warning. Cleaning supplies, as well as medicines, must be locked up or put out of reach. Consider moving all medicines and cleaning products to a high cupboard in the kitchen where they'll be safer and where children are apt to be more carefully supervised.

While toilet tissue can't be considered dangerous, be aware that for about a year "flushing fascination" may cause waste and perhaps even pipe clogging. Many parents keep toilet tissue off the holder during this period or discourage waste by keeping a rubber band around the roll.

- Replace childproof caps on medicine carefully and promptly after use. Save caps you're through with; often they'll fit on other bottles or jars you want to keep children from getting into.

- Keep the bathroom off limits for a small child by securing a bolt or hook-and-eye screws high up on the outside of the door.

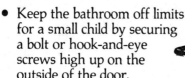

- Drape a towel over the top of the bathroom door to keep children from shutting it tightly and locking themselves in. Or stick tape across the doorknob bolt so it won't slip into the door jamb.

- And keep handy outside the door the key or a tool with which you can unlock it.

- Remove the bathroom doorknob altogether if it's one that doesn't unlock from the outside and you don't want to install another.

- Stick nonslip appliqués or strips to the bottom of the bathtub to prevent falls, or use a bathtub mat.

- Use plastic or paper drinking cups rather than breakable glass ones.

- Take the phone off the hook while you are bathing your child so ringing won't tempt you to leave him or her alone in the tub.

The children's rooms

- Check often for loose eyes on stuffed toys and for parts of other toys that might come off.

- Throw out broken toys, for safety's sake.

- Use open, stackable cubes or vegetable bins for storing clothes to make access easy for a child and to eliminate the possibility of the child pulling out a drawer on himself or herself.

- Secure your child's bureau or heavy bookcase to the wall with hook-and-eye screws to keep a climber from tipping them over.

- Glue suction cups or small blocks of cork on the undersides of the corners of a toy chest lid to avoid smashed fingers. Or install a pneumatic door spring (as on screen and storm doors) to make the lid open more easily and close slowly. Better yet, store toys behind sliding doors or on open shelving.

- Don't place a crib or other furniture that can be climbed on near a window.

Graduating to the big bed

- Let your child start to use a pillow while still in the crib — it will help him or her learn to "center" the body while asleep.

- Lower the side of the crib and put a stool beside it for a young walker who is about to graduate to a big bed. It's better to help your child climb out safely than to risk a fall.

- Push one side of the big bed against the wall for a recent crib graduate. Put a crib mattress on the floor next to the open side to cushion an accidental fall. Or use a removable side rail on that side for a few weeks.

- Turn the blanket crosswise, allowing for extra tuck-in along the mattress length.

- Roll two blankets and put one under each side of the mattress, lengthwise, to make a small "valley" for the child to sleep in.

If a Product Causes Injury ...

The U.S. Consumer Product Safety Commission is the place to call if your child is injured through the use of any product or if you have questions about the safety of any piece of equipment or furniture. In the Continental U.S. except for Maryland: 800-638-8326. In Maryland: 800-492-8363. In Alaska, Hawaii, Puerto Rico and the Virgin Islands: 800-638-8333. In Canada, write the Department of Consumer and Corporate Affairs, Place du Portage, Hull, Quebec K1A 0C9. Or call 613-977-1670.

Doors and windows

- Childproof windows with gratings or heavy screen. In some apartments, you can use window brackets that allow windows to open only a few inches.

- Open windows from the top if possible.

- Put decals at child's eye level on sliding glass doors as reminders that they ARE glass, not open space.

- Attach a bell to a door that a small child can open to give you a warning if he or she wanders out.

- Fasten an old sock over the doorknob with a rubber band. Adults can squeeze hard enough to turn the knob; small children can't.

- Put hook-and-eye screws high up on the outsides of doors to older children's rooms or others you don't want toddlers to go into. (Caution: children can be locked IN, also, by older siblings who are "just playing" or by lazy sitters.) Use the screws also on screen doors, but of course they'll only work in wood, so choose a wooden door instead of a metal one if you have the option and want to do this.

- Consider installing Dutch doors in certain areas, such as a laundry-workshop adjacent to a playroom. Children can be kept out of a dangerous area, yet a parent working there can still observe and supervise.

- Attach a flat curtain rod at child's height to a screen door that you WANT a child to be able to push open to keep the screen from being pushed out.

Stairways

- Put up a swinging gate at the top of the stairs; it can be secured when little ones are on the loose and open when you want it that way.

- Teach toddlers to crawl downstairs backwards and to get down from furniture backwards.

- Attach a rope to the lower rung of the stairway bannisters so a climbing child can grasp it for help in climbing.

Electricity

- You can simply be sure that furniture is placed in front of every electrical outlet in your house, but it's better to cover the outlets themselves. Start by covering them with strong, clear tape. When your child shows interest in removing it, graduate to pronged plastic caps, available at hardware stores.

- Wind up excess length of plugged-in cords and fasten with rubber bands or twist 'ems to keep your child from sucking or chewing on them and risking a bad mouth burn.

- Buy covers that lock plugs INTO outlets so children can't pull plugs out.

- Tape electric cords against walls to prevent tripping over them.

All around the house

- Don't assume that squeezing books tightly into a bookcase will keep a determined toddler from pulling them out. Chances are the bookcase will topple before the child gives up.

- Leave lower bookcase shelves and the shelf under the television stand open for toys and children's books — your possessions can be returned to their proper places in a few years.

- Cover the pointed tops in expandable gates with old socks so a toddler won't get scratched on them.

- Cover the rods used for handles and pedals of rocking horses with the kind of rubber tips you use for chair legs to make them less dangerous. Or use plastic bike handles with formed grips.

- Apply a foam rubber strip with adhesive backing (used for insulation) to the rounds of a baby's walker to protect your furniture. The foam sticks to itself, so can be wrapped around twice.

- Turn a desk with its drawers to the wall — use only the surface.

- Glue small cork blocks or suction cups at each end of the piano keyboard lid to prevent smashed fingers.

- Pull chairs up close to the dining table so that a toddler can't climb up on them.

- Pick up your active baby and take him or her along with you when you leave a room to answer the phone or the doorbell; it takes only a minute for a child to get into trouble.

- Or at least put the baby in the infant seat INSIDE the playpen when you must leave a baby and a toddler in a room alone together. Or put the toddler in the playpen!

- And put the Christmas tree inside the playpen to keep it out of a toddler's reach.

- DON'T EVER let a child run with a popsicle or lollipop stick, or any other such object, in his or her mouth.

- NEVER leave a plastic bag where a child can play with it — suffocation can result. And when you throw a plastic bag away, be doubly safe and tie knots in it.

- Hold down contact points on the phone with wide rubber bands to keep a child from "disconnecting" you or accidentally dialing South Africa.

- Hang the phone cord on a cup hook screwed into the wall above the phone so your child can't pull on it.

Preventing Accidental Poisoning

The most common causes of poisoning in children six and under are, in order, drugs, plants, personal care products and household cleaners. Children should be supervised especially carefully before meal times — they're more liable to sample foreign substances when they're hungry. Teach your child early to say "ahhh"; you may get a chance to see what's in a mouth and pull it out before harm is done. Careful parents keep the number of their nearest poison control centers posted by every phone in the house.

To find the number of your nearest poison control center in the U.S., contact the National Poison Center Network, 125 DeSoto Street, Pittsburgh, PA 15213, 412-681-6669. The Network will send you a dozen Mr. Yuk stickers and a home-teaching unit on poison prevention for $1, to cover postage. The ugly Mr. Yuk has proved far more effective in controlling accidental poisoning than the traditional skull-and-crossbones symbol.

For poison control information in Canada, write the Department of Health and Welfare, Brooke Clarton Boulevard, Ottawa, Ontario K1A 0K9, or call 613-922-0979.

Parents should keep ipecac (available from pharmacies without a prescription) on hand to induce vomiting — but use it ONLY if directed to do so by the poison center or a doctor. Ipecac is sold in bottles that contain two tablespoons; children under six are given only one tablespoon. The drug's shelf life is five years.

SAFETY OUTSIDE

A whole new set of hazards presents itself to a child outdoors and away from home. There are attractive things to taste, unfamiliar settings to investigate, interesting equipment to experiment with and dangerous streets to cross. There's often also a possibility of getting lost.

You might consider attaching a trucker's side-view mirror to an appropriate spot outside your kitchen window to keep a play area in your line of sight, when children first begin to play outside alone.

In the yard

- Glue a rubber bathmat or stick nonslip bathtub strips onto a swing seat to prevent your child from slipping off.

- Don't use ordinary clothesline for homemade swing ropes; it's not strong enough. Nylon, sisal or polyethylene ropes are better.

- Cover swing chains with sections of garden hose to avoid torn clothes and provide a more comfortable grip.

- Wrap adhesive or electrical tape around swing chains, over the hose, at the level a child should grip, to be sure he or she has the correct balance.

- Spread four to six inches of loose material such as pine bark nuggets, sand or shredded tires under the swings and other playground equipment to cushion falls.

- Cover exposed screws and bolts with caps or tape; pinch the ends of S-hooks together with pliers so they can't catch a child's skin or clothing.

- Check your own outdoor equipment for safety regularly and also check playground equipment supplied by your apartment or at your local park.

- Place an extension ladder across the driveway a few feet from the end to keep preschoolers from riding trikes into the street. Or paint a red stripe across the driveway as a reminder.

- Don't buy plastic riding toys on which seams go around the wheels — the seams will eventually split and a nasty fall could result.

In the car

There is NO SAFE ALTERNATIVE to an approved, reliable car restraint — a car seat for a baby or small child under about 40 pounds or four years old, or a seat belt for an older child. Parents who may be tempted to transport a baby in a car bed or portable crib and to let older children romp in the back of a station wagon must be warned that they're tempting fate. Children usually accept safety habits well if they are established right from the start and NEVER varied — and if parents and other adults in the car set good examples by always buckling up. To protect your auto upholstery, put a strip of heavy vinyl carpet runner under the car seat.

- Teach children an auto safety routine: an adult says, "Hands up — doors closed and locked. Fasten belts. Blast off!" An older child can be appointed "First Mate" to see that the procedure is carried out correctly.

- Choose a car seat that lets a toddler sit high enough to see out of the window.

- Pull over to the side of the road if there's screaming or fighting in the car. Stay there until everyone settles down.

- Spread a light-colored bassinet sheet, towel or receiving blanket over a car seat in the summer to avoid a "hot seat" that can cause second-degree burns to a child's tender skin. When the child is old enough to use a seat belt, keep a towel in the car for the same purpose.

- Put a hat on a small child to shield his or her eyes from the sun in the car. Or glue strips of Velcro above side windows, sew Velcro to one edge of a towel and attach it to cover the too-bright window. Or apply "solar film" to the window on the side of the car the seat is set up on.

- Transport any sharp or heavy object in the car trunk, not in the passenger area.

- Never let a child play with the controls of a car; get a play steering wheel and horn combination that snaps onto a car seat for one who loves to "drive."

- Never leave children unattended in a car and don't leave the car motor running when children are playing near the car.

GETTING CHORES DONE

B.C. (Before Children), when you could work without interruption, you may have had the best-kept house in town. That's not possible with little kids around. "A clean house shows a life misspent" is a slogan you may wish to adopt.

Keeping kids out of the way

You can try to work "around" your kids, stopping when you must and pressing on when you can. You can let them "help" you (remember that sometimes they're really learning!). Or you can try to keep them out of the way entirely by farming them out or hiring a sitter (less expensive than cleaning help, and a good way to check out a new sitter). The cardinal rule for many parents is that naptime and bedtime are NOT the signals for work to begin — they're for PRIVATE TIME!

- Put your baby in a padded laundry basket or small cardboard box with a few toys and let him or her travel with you from room to room as you work. It's a good way for a baby to practice sitting for short periods of time.

- Let the parent who's not doing the housework take over the child entertaining.

- Put the baby in a backpack. He or she will be in the desired place (near you), and your hands will be free to work.

- Assign your child his or her own kitchen drawer or cupboard stocked with assorted plastic containers, cans and other safe kitchen items.

- Allow your child to play in water in the sink while you work in the kitchen — but do it on the day you plan to wash the floor!

- Give a small child a short piece of cellophane or masking tape to play with if you want a few minutes of quiet time to work or talk on the phone. Or put a dab of baby lotion on the highchair tray to keep your child busy.

- Curb a child's impatience for "the cake to be done" or "playtime with Mom" to come by setting a timer and letting him or her watch it run down.

- Hang a mirror on the wall in the kitchen so that you can see children in the next room. (This lends credence to the "eyes-in-the-back-of-the-head" myth.)

Encouraging neatness

- Keep a clean new dustpan in the toy box. A child can scoop up small objects with it. Or let the child gather up toys with a shag rug rake.

- Have a child who gets an allowance pay you a penny for each toy or article of clothing you pick up and store in a big box or bag until payment is collected. Or have him or her do a special chore for the return of a toy.

- Or let anything you have to pick up simply DISAPPEAR for a time.

- Offer to pick up your child's toys occasionally, in return for him or her doing one of your simpler chores.

- Try working along with the child sometimes; it's more fun to work with company than alone.

- Encourage picking up right after an activity instead of at the end of the day to make the task less overwhelming.

- Have visiting friends help with the picking up before they leave.

- Help the kids put their things away on open shelving by drawing labels for items and taping them on the proper shelves.

- Install a basketball ring over the kids' laundry hamper to provide an incentive for tossing in soiled clothes.

- Keep a tall, narrow plastic container in each child's closet for personal storage of soiled clothes, or hang a colorful pillowcase with loops sewn onto it on the back of a door for laundry.

- Provide a visible example of neatness by putting YOUR things away, too.

Kids really helping

Even very small children can help around the house, if you're patient and don't expect perfection. It's important to remember to stress the importance of ALL work, to express appreciation for any job well done and to switch assignments occasionally to avoid boredom. If you're cheerful at your work and try to find some humor in humdrum activities, the kids will probably follow suit. Rewards inspire help, too, and the "house fairy" may visit often to leave treats for good workers. Just be sure to make it a firm rule NEVER to redo work a child (or your mate!) has done. Willing help will be hard to come by if you do.

- Give a child a card with a smiling face sticker on it, or another token, to put in a place where he or she has done an unasked chore or favor. Then be sure to notice the card and praise the child.

- Put a time limit on chores, or time them with a timer or a record on the stereo, to make work seem to have an end. Or have a race to see who can finish a chore first, if the quality of the work isn't really important.

- Try printing titles of jobs on slips of paper when there's a lot to do and you want everyone to pitch in. Include some that say, "Hop on one foot," and "Eat one cookie." For little kids, you can draw pictures that illustrate such jobs as "feed the dog" and "set the table."

- Give a reason for cleaning up and set a deadline: "before Daddy comes home" or "by lunch time." Not having to "do it right now" gives a child a choice and makes a job seem to be something he or she wants to do.

- Let the child closest to the floor pick things up and give them to you or to an older child to put away, when picking up is a group project.

- Assign each child a specific number of items to pick up, and teach counting as the job gets done. Or let the child pick up items whose names begin with letters you call out, or which are the colors you name.

GETTING ORGANIZED

Saving time, money and trouble is something most parents want to do. To find a clever use for an item that's no longer needed for its original purpose... to protect a piece of furniture so that it outlasts its expected lifetime... to make a child's room a haven of comfort and convenience at little or no cost... all can give a feeling of accomplishment.

Something out of something else

- Use metal shower curtain rings as locks for yard gates.

- Use a baby's outgrown plastic tub for water play outdoors or indoors, with a big plastic tablecloth under it. Or use it for a portable toy box, indoors or out.

- Carpet playpen floors with new carpet scraps or samples, for comfort and warmth, or with vinyl scraps or samples for easy cleanup.

- Moisture proof a vinyl playpen pad by covering it with a piece of quilted material such as a mattress pad, or with a length of terrycloth.

- Mend a torn mesh playpen with dental floss or fishing line.

- Turn an old piano bench into a play table for children to sit at on low stools or chairs (overturned bakery containers or big ice cream buckets do fine!). It even offers storage space!

- Cut away part of the front and sides of a medium-sized plastic wastebasket, smooth the edges carefully and set a large pillow in the bottom for a bucket-type booster seat.

- Spread out an old window shade on the carpet for a floor cover where children are playing or coloring. A flannel-backed vinyl tablecloth works as well.

- Use a large old diaper pail as a laundry hamper.

- Use the old bottle sterilizer as a corn popper or as a steamer for corn on the cob, other vegetables, or clams. The hole in the cover prevents boil-overs.

Kids' rooms: walls

- Paint a growth chart on the wall for a visible, long-lasting record.

- Cut figures appropriate to a child's age and interests from self-adhesive vinyl. Press them onto a painted wall for economical "wallpaper."

- Cover a section of a wall with shelf paper for drawing or paint a wall or door with blackboard paint for a child to scribble on. Use a big old powder puff for an eraser. If crayon marks carry over onto a painted wall, remove them with toothpaste on a damp cloth.

- Or thumbtack plain oilcloth to the wall. It can be used as a blackboard, it wipes clean and it's easily replaced when worn. Kids love to draw and paint on artists' canvas, too, but it can't be washed clean.

- Make a bulletin board from the side of a large furniture or appliance carton. Trim neatly and add colorful masking tape or thin molding for a border.

- Put cork squares on the inside of the bedroom door — they serve the double purpose of muffling noise and providing bulletin board space.

Kids' rooms: furnishings

- Avoid shag rugs — dangerous objects, as well as food and gum, can be hidden in the pile. A low-pile, washable bathroom rug is practical for a small child's room, and indoor-outdoor carpeting makes a good play surface, too.

- Consider installing track lighting and avoid the problems of lamps which can be overturned.

- Suspend a discarded lamp shade from a ceiling light fixture and attach small, no-longer-played-with toys with fine wire or fishing line.

- Avoid bunk beds, at least until your child is dry all night. It's hard to change linens on both upper and lower bunks. You might wish to encourage the use of sleeping bags instead of sheets and blankets when you DO set up the bunks. At least get fitted top sheets as well as bottom ones, if you can find them (try a mail-order catalog), or make them, if they're not available.

- Speed up the chore of bunk bed-making by making fitted spreads from regular bedspreads and saving all that tuck-in. Use the extra fabric for pillow shams.

- Turn an old twin bed or crib mattress into an extra bed for sleep-over friends. It slides under a bed for storage.

- Use bean-bag chairs in kids' rooms, or big foam pillows that can serve as building material for forts as well as for sitting and tumbling. You might want to ban shoes in the bean-bag chair — a rip can be disastrous.

- Make more space for play, and make the room look bigger, by removing the closet door and putting the child's bureau inside the closet.

STORING STUFF

The number of THINGS a child accumulates seems to be in direct proportion to his or her age. The new baby's clothes and toys take up a lot of space, the toddler's even more. But, oh, the preschooler's stuff! It's worthwhile to spend a little time and effort on organization, especially if you want to encourage your child to take responsibility for his or her own belongings.

Kids' clothes

- Store small children's socks in the bottom halves of plastic egg cartons which have been carefully washed and set into drawers as dividers.

- Store underclothes, socks, T-shirts and other small items of clothing in stackable plastic bins that are open on the front. They're easier for children to use than heavy bureau drawers.

- Cut out pictures of clothing items and tape them on the appropriate drawers to help children locate and put away their clothes.

Closet hangups

- Make closet lights easy to turn on by tying bright colored spools to the pull-chains or cords.

- Make a clothes rod at child's height with a broom handle attached to the regular rod at each end with sturdy cord. The cord can be shortened to raise the rod as the child grows. Or use commercially made rod extenders, available in notions departments.

- Assign each person a coat hook and put up wicker bicycle baskets over each to hold caps, gloves and scarves.

- Or attach a metal shoe rack or cloth shoe bag to the wall inside or near the closet.

- Or glue clothespins with a hot glue gun to the inside of a closet door.

- Put a clothes hook low on the back of a child's bedroom door for pajamas and robe.

- Hang your umbrella stroller from a hook in a closet to keep it out of the way, or set it in your umbrella holder or a tall basket near the front door.

Kids' toys

Of course the trick is to accumulate the minimum — especially of toys with a million pieces. What you don't have ... you don't have to store. How simple it sounds!

- Remember that horizontal storage is better than vertical for toys; small items get lost and sometimes broken at the bottom of big chests or boxes.

- Build shelves of bricks and boards, but not so high that there's danger of their toppling. The area underneath makes a nice "garage" for pull toys and cars and the shelves are for books and toys.

- Put up a wooden pole with pegs, or an expandable metal plant pole, from floor to ceiling. Sew loops on stuffed animals and hang them on the pegs for neatness and decorativeness, too.

- Or attach inexpensive fishnet in folds to the wall to give each stuffed animal its own "cage."

- Attach hardware to hinge a wooden stair step and put a floor under the step to give you a nice little cupboard for toys or boots.

- Attach strips of Velcro horizontally on walls at child's height and sew or glue other strips on toys. The child "sticks" his or her toys away.

- Store a few toys in a plastic clothes basket, which even a small child can easily pull from room to room for playing and for quick pick-ups. (And when your child is through with it, you can use it for your own purposes.)

Organizers for Toys

- A small suitcase.
- A large mailbox.
- The old bassinet.
- Laundry bags, hung from wall hooks.
- Large, clear sweater boxes.
- Baskets, attached to the wall.
- Fishing tackle boxes.
- A rolling mesh or plastic basket cart.
- Stackable plastic vegetable bins.
- A plastic dish drainer (for books and records; the silverware section will hold pencils and crayons).
- Three, five or seven 46-ounce cans or plastic ice cream buckets, glued together with open ends facing the same way, and spray painted. Set the assembly on its side, like a wine rack, to hold small toys or art materials.
- A large plastic garbage can with a swing lid.
- Large cardboard ice cream containers.
- Large heavy boxes cut down and covered with contact paper or wallpaper.
- Disposable diaper boxes.

Chapter 5

The Challenge of Parenting

Perhaps the greatest challenge of parenting is to help our children to become social human beings. We want them to become secure ... competent ... well-adjusted ... polite ... and independent human beings, but those qualities can't be developed by simply following a formula. Our children's unique personalities and our own, plus all the other factors in our particular situations, combine to further complicate the already complicated process of growing up.

MANNERS

Setting a good example in social situations is important. "Do as I say, not as I do," doesn't wash, even with little children. In order to cut down the use of NO in front of others (and alone at home, too), some parents try to say YES, with qualifications. "Yes, you may have a cookie — after dinner." "Yes, you may play outdoors — after your nap."

Being quiet

- Choose front-row seats at church services or other gatherings where children are apt to be noisy or fidgety. Knowing they can be seen helps some behave well, and most enjoy being able to see what's going on.

- Or sit in back, where you can make a quick getaway if necessary. Some say to exit only when absolutely necessary and to return as soon as potty duty has been accomplished or screaming has stopped.

- Seat a child between two adults at a meeting or service.

- Teach your child to whisper — a technique that must be learned — before you take him or her to places where talking aloud isn't possible. There's "outside" and "inside" talking, too — loud and soft.

- Find little jobs for children to do when they must be quiet in church or at meetings. They may keep track of how many times the rabbi or minister says "God," or they may count the number of children in each row of seats.

- Bring an assortment of quiet toys or objects in a small bag for a child to play with at a meeting or service and let him or her carry them. One possibility is a stack of fabric scraps pinned together. Or take a spool of thread along and break off short lengths for your child to play with, if he or she is old enough not to try to eat them.

- If you want to bring a "quiet food," try raisins.

Table talk

- Teach children to modulate their voices by recording them on tape and playing it back so they can hear their own stridency.

- Set up a series of signals for making corrections in table manners. Quietly saying, "Twenty-two," for example, is not annoying to children and makes correcting them away from home less obvious. (But some parents say this practice leads to a game for older children, who sometimes enjoy putting their parents through a little exercise in calling numbers.)

The proper response

- Refuse to respond to "huh?" once you've explained "pardon me?" Wait for "please," "thank you" and "excuse me" until they're habitual.

- Don't let go of an item you're offering your child until you hear "please" or "thank you."

- Apologize for your own lapses and ask children to do the same.

Telephone interruptions

You can minimize phone calls while your child is in the interrupting stage ... you can have little talks about manners ...

you can pace about, maintaining order while you're talking, holding an extra long phone cord above your head. But the interruptions probably won't really stop until your child is old enough to make and receive calls and realizes the importance of quiet while someone's on the phone. In the meantime, there are things to try.

- Take advantage of the time to hold and cuddle your child.

- Allow water play in the sink, if you're talking in the kitchen and can keep an eye on the child.

- Keep a special box of toys or a pad of paper and a few crayons near the phone, to be played with only while you're talking.

- Get your child a toy phone to talk on while you're on YOUR phone.

- Teach the child to raise a hand or to place it on his or her head if it's really necessary to interrupt you. You can terminate your conversation or ask the party to hold for a moment while you take care of the child.

- Try to help your child know when you MUST NOT be interrupted. Stand up for uninterruptible calls; sit down for calls when it won't matter.

- SOMETIMES (you'll be sorry if you allow it to become a habit!) let the child say hello to your caller, if it's someone like Grandma, who won't mind.

- Adjust your phoning time when you can to make calls during naptime, and ask callers to call back then.

TANTRUMS

Most parents believe it's best to ignore tantrums whenever possible, because when there's no audience, there's no need to perform. Many caution, though, that it's important not to ignore the CHILD. They ask themselves if they're enforcing too-rigid standards, holding too-high expectations or perhaps simply not giving enough TLC. Try, too, to avoid the tantrum point: keep your child from becoming overtired or frustrated. Giving a little help with a toy that won't work, insisting on a short rest or offering a little snack — any of the three may avert the tantrum if you can see it coming.

Dealing with temper tantrums

- Let your child scream to his or her heart's content sometimes (outdoors, perhaps, if you live in the country). Everybody needs to let off steam occasionally.

- If your discipline precipitated the tantrum, tell the child firmly that the rule still stands and that he or she will have to deal with the tantrum alone; then ignore the child.

- Try to distract the child by doing or saying something unusual or silly. You might even stage your own mock tantrum. Or switch the light off and on rapidly, another attention-getter. Some parents say to pour a glass of water over a child's head for REAL drama!

- Disappear! If you're in another room, you'll feel better, and the tantrum will probably be short-lived. If the child follows you, move again.

- Stop breath-holding during a tantrum, if it continues until you're worried about cyanosis (lack of oxygen to the brain), by blowing gently into the child's face, dashing a small amount of cold water on the face or applying a cold cloth. Children usually do come out of this on their own.

- Escort your child calmly to the car or a restroom if a tantrum begins when you're away from home. When the tantrum subsides, return to the business at hand. If you can't leave, simply let the tantrum continue and grit your teeth. Most of the adults who see it have probably been parents of tantrum tots, too.

Handling inappropriate behavior

Behavior you don't like is occurring. If it's something that's just "getting to you" or that's basically harmless to life and limb and furnishings, you may decide to ignore it and allow logical consequences to follow. If you're making an effort not to yell at your child, stand face to face with him or her — you'll find it virtually impossible to scream.

- Whisper, if it's noisy, and the child may stop to listen.

- Set a timer for when the behavior must stop. Or start counting aloud, being sure the child knows how far you will count. And be prepared to do something at the end of the time; empty threats don't work.

- Call out a funny magic phrase ("Un-gah-wah!"), which is ALWAYS your family secret signal to STOP, whatever activity is going on. Remember to use it sometimes in positive situations, such as at street crossings, and be prepared to have it used back to you.

- Congratulate your child on his or her control and good sense when the misbehavior stops.

- Designate a "time out" place or chair where the child must stay when behavior is out of line and set a timer for perhaps three to five minutes. This not only ends the behavior; it also gives the child an out, stopping the momentum, which may have gotten out of control.

Calming an angry child

- Hold a small child tightly; rock and sing. Express your love in terms of increasing largeness: "My love for you is as big as a flower ... as big as a teacup ... as big as a bush," and try to get him or her involved in thinking up bigger and bigger things.

- Whisper in his or her ear. Screaming will usually stop, and if you can think of something really good to whisper, the child's mood may change.

- Tell your child there's a smile inside, and if it's not let out, it will turn to a giggle. It will, often. Or mimic your child, exaggeratedly, and say, "No laughing!" (This, of course, is ignoring the anger, so, when it's over, talk about it with your child.)

- "Scold" a piece of furniture or a toy that causes trouble for your child. He or she will probably end up laughing.

- "Lend" your child a hug and a kiss when things are going well; call in the "loan" when anger strikes. This gives the child a chance to feel warmth and calm down so you can talk about it.

Helping a child vent anger

Children, like adults, shouldn't be required to hold anger in. You may want to talk with your child about his or her anger, encouraging the use of words to express it, and showing your understanding. But remember that doing something physical may be more helpful for the child than anything else.

- Encourage your child to vent anger physically by running around outdoors, punching a big batch of play dough or hitting a tree with a stick.

- Teach the child to count to five in a LOUD, ANGRY voice, to play an ANGRY song on a musical instrument or to dance an ANGRY dance.

- Or shout something loud WITH your child, and let your voices drop ... drop ... until there's silence.

- Ask an angry child to draw a picture showing how he or she feels, a creative way to relieve feelings.

SIBLING RIVALRY

The only sure cure for sibling rivalry is to have only one child; a certain amount of rivalry, jealousy and squabbling is normal between siblings. It's not possible to make anyone stop feeling certain emotions like hate and the need to win. Growing up knowing that there are times you dislike someone you love is realistic and healthy.

It's usually best to let the children work things out themselves, since much fighting is done mainly to prod parents into doing SOMETHING. Of course, there are times when you must interfere for safety's sake — and others when you just can't stand any more fighting!

Fair is fair

- Be sure your children have rights to their OWN things. It's hard to share if they're not secure and guilt-free about ownership. Allow them NOT to share, if they wish.

- Don't label a child "selfish" or show disapproval over unwillingness to share. Make a point of sharing, yourself, and be sure your children see you doing it.

- Tell a child who doesn't want to share, "When you are finished, Dan may have it." This lets the child know someone's waiting, but eliminates the distress of giving up the toy immediately.

- Or set a timer to sound off when it's time to exchange toys.

- Let one child cut the cake or divide the orange sections and the other get first pick when they're fighting about fairness.

- Or assign each child a special day or days (like Monday, Wednesday, Friday) when he or she may make certain decisions, select menus, be first at everything.

- Play the "stone game": put a small stone in one hand, and the child who picks the right one gets first choice.

- Avoid fights over similar objects such as pails and shovels, balls and such by assigning a color to each child and always trying to buy those types of items in the assigned colors.

- Divide the bedroom shared by squabblers with a bookcase and divide the closet by painting half one color and the other half another.

Changing the pace

- Suggest a new activity when the kids are squabbling a lot. Boredom often leads to quarrels.

- Try distraction when you see that an older child is about to attack a younger one: "Quick, I need you! Please come help me."

- Try spraying glass cleaner on the inside and outside of a sliding glass door or low first-floor windows. Put one angry child on each side with a dry cloth. By the time the glass is dry, the kids will be laughing.

- Make the children hug each other when they fight. Next time they'll think twice — no one wants to hug a sibling he or she is angry with.

- End a verbal argument by having kids SING their complaints to each other.

- Ask the kids for ideas to solve the problem. Let them think of special ways they can accommodate each other. Even if the ideas aren't workable, the kids will be involved in subsequent action.

- Get up and leave the house, if you can, or at least consider the bathroom as a refuge. Like temper tantrums, fighting often stops when there's no audience.

End of options

- Send each of two quarreling children to a different corner of the room and sit them down facing each other. They must stay put until they give each other "permission" to leave. Negotiations usually lead to peace.

- Or have each child tell five things that he or she thinks are nice qualities or actions of the other. Mutual compliments often end the war.

- Force a compromise by removing the object of disagreement or separating the children.

"KICKING" HABITS

Habits that parents don't like aren't necessarily bad ones — more often they're just very annoying. Some are established as responses to frustration or anxiety, others as tension-relievers to provide security in a confusing world. Some parents find that ignoring a habit helps, if no one is being hurt, but others try to get to the bottom of things. They chart the habit, noting when and under what circumstances it takes place; then they work to avoid those situations or help the child learn to cope with them.

Some try distraction but they warn that the habit may be reinforced if the child sees it as a way to get attention. Remember, at least, that YOU can't break a child's habit — you can only help the CHILD break it.

The pacifier

- Put pickle juice or something else sour or bitter on the pacifier — it won't taste good.

- LOSE the pacifier of a child 18 months or older. At that age, he or she will probably understand the concept of losing things and won't question the fact that the crutch is gone.

- Start a little hole in the pacifier and enlarge it a bit every few days until the "taste" and shape are no longer appealing.

- Tell the child that when this "last" pacifier is lost or worn out, there will be no more. The advance notice may make the end easier.

- Try to coordinate giving up the pacifier with giving up the regular nap, if it's possible. (But remember that if you get the child to give up the pacifier, the nap may go, too, whether you like it or not!) A very tired child will go to sleep quickly at night and probably won't miss the pacifier much.

Biting

Children bite for different reasons, usually depending upon their ages. For a baby, biting may simply be a new tactile experience. The child who bites in anger or frustration usually outgrows the habit when he or she is old enough to verbalize the problems. Then, too, there is the possibility that a child is imitating another biter — human or otherwise. Whatever the cause, VIGILANCE is recommended until the habit is outgrown or "cured."

- Pinch the child's nose shut. He or she will release the victim.

- Remove the child from your lap or the room, explaining that biting is not acceptable.

- Say, "NO BITING," perhaps while holding the child's jaw on either side of the mouth with thumb and index finger and applying light pressure.

- Dramatize your pain and sorrow; the child's sympathy may rise to the top. (If the child seems to think this is a marvelous game — try another tactic!)

- Try giving the child something he or she CAN bite, such as a rubber toy or soft doll. Or an apple or a bagel!

- Put the child's arm in his or her mouth and insist on a "self-bite" to show how much it really hurts.

- Say, "Oh, so you want to play the biting game!" if you decide to bite back — gently.

Thumb-sucking

Many parents say, "DON'T TRY TO STOP IT; thumb-sucking fulfills a need for comfort and security." Some dentists feel that, if it's continued for a long time, thumb-sucking or finger-sucking can change the shape of a child's mouth and put permanent teeth out of alignment — a good reason for regular dental checkups. If you want to see it stopped, there are things to try.

- Try giving a baby a pacifier as a substitute. Some dentists say the Nuk pacifier will not ruin tooth alignment.

- Try some physical means of stopping the thumb-sucking, such as a bad-tasting solution that you buy at the drugstore. (Some parents caution that if a child rubs his or her eyes, the stuff will sting.)

- Sew mitts to pajama sleeves or buy or make finger puppets for the child to wear for sleeping.

- Put a kiss in each of your child's hands at bedtime and tell him or her to hold them closed all night to keep the kisses in.

- Restrict thumb-sucking for an older child to his or her own room. The desire can then be indulged, and you won't have to see it. Chances are that keeping you company in the rest of the house will become more important than the habit.

- Ask your dentist to warn the child about possible future dental problems, if he or she agrees that they may follow. The voice of a "neutral party" often carries more weight than that of a parent.

Dawdling

Dawdling is just a form of negativism, which most children pick up at age two to three. Be patient — it passes.

- Set a timer in a child's room and make it a game for him or her to be washed and dressed by the time it goes off.

- Get your child an alarm clock to help instill a sense of responsibility about getting up. Be lavish with praise when responsibility is shown.

- Don't serve breakfast to a child still in pajamas; one who's dressed before eating is ready to go!

- Don't turn on television until the child is dressed, in order to keep distractions to a minimum.

- Help your child hurry by reminding him or her of the fun and good things that may happen during the day.

- Let a dawdler miss an activity, if that's possible to arrange. Chances are that the child will be ready the next time.

FEARS AND TEARS

The apparent fear that developing babies show by turning away from anyone other than a parent is nothing to apologize for or to worry about — it's a sign of expanding mental and emotional reaction. Toddlers and older children learn fear when they realize that they can't control some things. They may be afraid of being hurt or of pain, or of being abandoned at bedtime or when left with a sitter. Teasing and shaming a fearful child may cause him or her to hide the fear behind belligerence or to give up and become withdrawn. It's important to LISTEN carefully to a child to find out exactly what he or she is afraid of.

Facing up to fears

- Reintroduce an eight- or nine-month-old child to the vacuum cleaner, if fear of it develops. Carry the child with you as you vacuum; guide his or her hand to the on-off switch; let the child push with you.

- Do something physical about irrational fears of such things as "monsters," say parents who think magical things can only be dealt with magically. Spray them away with a spray can or cologne spray (the child will smell "monster repellant" after you're gone); blow them out the window; flush them down the toilet; throw them out in the garbage; have the family pet come in to eat them; or recite a homemade incantation against them before leaving the room. (Some parents disagree — they say that such actions reinforce the fear, because a parent seems to believe in them, too. They feel that saying, "There are no monsters, except in make-believe," is better.)

- Treat all fears seriously, doing what you can to alleviate them. For example, if a child is afraid of shadows on the wall caused by outside traffic, take the trouble to move his or her bed to a "safer" wall or to get an opaque shade.

- Rehearse events that scare your child. Play "what if," and discuss what a child should do in case of getting lost, being in an auto accident or having a parent get sick.

- Face up to fear. Admit that you — and all adults — feel afraid sometimes. Tell your child about fears you had as a child and how you overcame them. Or ask the child's grandparents to tell about your fears.

- Don't discourage your child if he or she needs a "security blanket" or other favorite object to feel safe.

The Security Blanket

Don't let your child think the blanket or other "lovey" he or she becomes attached to is BAD. Such security objects help ease the transition to independence and symbolize your child's ability to develop an interest in things outside himself or herself.

- Cut a favorite blanket in half — early, as soon as the child becomes attached to it — and whisk the dirty half away for laundering when he or she doesn't see you. With luck, the child will never realize there are two blankets.
- Try to promote a diaper as the security blanket — there's always one available and it's always clean.
- Or cut up one of your old nightgowns into small pieces, if your child has always loved their softness. The pieces won't drag on the floor and there'll be a good supply of clean ones.
- Consider saving the shreds of a security blanket, once it's been discarded — they've become the base of more than one wedding bouquet.

Fear of the dark

- Take a night walk up and down your block in good weather to teach a child that the dark is magical, not spooky. Or lie on a blanket in your yard or the park, looking at the stars, watching for fireflies, listening to night sounds.

- Remember that there's no law that a child can't sleep with the light on. You can provide a nightlight easily by replacing the bulb in a regular lamp with a small colored bulb. Or consider a lighted fish tank that the child can watch until he or she falls asleep.

- Give the child a wind-up music box; play a tape of soft music; or turn on a radio to distract him or her.

Nightmares

- Be sure a child who has had a bad dream or a nightmare is completely awake. Talk to him or her soothingly and reassuringly; insist on an answer that shows he or she is not still half asleep.

- Take the child to the bathroom; it's probably a good idea anyway, and it will assure complete wakefulness.

- Talk just a little about the dream, explaining that it was ONLY a dream and not reality. The next day, talk more about it and discuss the fact that dreams are marvelous experiences over which a person can have control. If something's chasing you, for example, you can turn around and chase IT.

Fear of thunder

- Play records of marching music to cheer a child afraid of a thunderstorm. The loudness of the music will drown out the thunder, and marching will give him or her something active to do.

- BOOM back at thunder.

- Or play a game, like seeing if you and the child can sing a whole verse of a song or recite the whole alphabet before the next thunderclap.

Leavetaking, with tears

There are parents who patiently accept the inconvenience of staying home with a child until he or she feels totally secure about being left with a sitter. Others say that you shouldn't feel guilty about going out — both parents and children are happier with occasional separations. Children are smart enough to pick up on your guilt and play "poor me," they say. Some sneak out while the child is occupied; others say, "NEVER do that!" Many do try to leave for only a short period of time when a new sitter is on duty.

- Get the sitter to come a half-hour or so early so that an activity can be started before you go and the child will be busy.

- Spend a few minutes with the child before you leave, and try not to have to rush off hurriedly.

- Use a set goodbye ritual, including a hug and kiss and such things as waving goodbye from the doorway or window or honking the car horn as you pull away.

- Kiss the child's palm and close his or her fingers into a fist, explaining that, if there's a need for a kiss, there's one in there, ready and waiting.

- Keep family pictures handy so the sitter can look at them with your child. The child will feel secure about his or her background and "belonging."

- Try to be back when you've said you will be, and remind the child that you always come back. Call if you're delayed and explain the problem to your child in person if he or she is old enough to talk on the phone.

- Tell a child who doesn't understand about time that you'll be back "after snack time" instead of "in three hours." For a child who's a little older, set a clock with the time you'll be back so that he or she can compare it with one that's running.

- Leave your child at a sitter's house with a security blanket, book or favorite toy.

- Forewarn the child about your going, say some parents, even days ahead if possible. Talk about who will be caring for him or her and what exciting things may be done, but be sure not to promise something that hasn't been arranged in advance with the sitter.

DEVELOPING SELF-ESTEEM

Parents who want their children to develop high self-esteem make a point of treating them with respect and courtesy; they don't reserve "please," "thank you" and "I'm sorry" for adults. They say that they don't belittle their children and that they correct or punish them in private, when they can, to help their kids save face. And they say, "Don't take it all too seriously — no single incident will shape your child's character!"

Showing respect

- Knock at your child's closed door and wait for an invitation to enter. Your child should return the courtesy to you.

- Borrow a child's things only after asking, as he or she must before borrowing yours. If you borrow a little money, give the child an official I.O.U. to make the transaction "legal."

- Let your child know very clearly, when necessary, that it is his or her BEHAVIOR that is naughty or rude. Say, "That's a bad way to act," not, "You are a bad child."

- Soften a criticism, when you must criticize, by giving your child a compliment before and after it.

- Take the time to introduce your children to others, as you do for adults.

Making children feel special

- Use your child's name often in conversation and make use of nicknames only if he or she really likes them. And use the name in other ways — wooden letters on the wall of the child's room, a sign on the door, a puzzle, a homemade placemat.

- Make each child a SPECIALIST in the family — your "favorite two-year-old," the "exercise leader" or the "nature scout." (Some parents disagree with this suggestion and the next one, saying that other children feel left out. They suggest instead that parents should praise a child's ACTIONS and avoid even good labels.)

- Share a special secret with each child. It could be a "middle child" club, if both parent and child qualify, or a code word that no one else knows. (Those who disagree with this suggestion try to plan daily one-to-one sessions with each child instead.)

- Tell your child stories in which he or she is the hero. Or investigate the specially printed, personalized books that use the names of the child, siblings, friends and pets.

- Write about your child...with your child. Keep a joint diary, let the child draw illustrations, and cover the pages with clear contact paper to preserve them. Sometimes read a page or two to the child at bedtime.

- Share baby record books and photo albums with children, so that they can enjoy their own growth and development.

- Keep a regular "baby" drawer or box into which you drop an anecdotal record of your child's life several times a year and perhaps even a letter you wrote to the unborn child while you were pregnant. The drawer or box serves as a place to store the child's artwork as he or she grows older, and going through everything once or twice a year is fun for all.

- Tape-record your child's voice, as he or she sings, recites or just converses with you, and play it back with your child, expressing your delight again at his or her verbal skills.

- Let the kids entertain you with plays they make up. Give a child a wooden spoon or a single beater from a mixer as a "microphone" and prepare to clap a lot as he or she hams it up.

- Surprise your child with a large, inexpensive blowup of a favorite photo of himself or herself.

Specials for fathers

In spite of the fact that DADA is one of the first words a baby learns (often inspired by MAMA, who wants to make Dad feel good), fathers often spend comparatively little time with their children when they're small. Today more and more fathers are finding that they want to have a more meaningful influence on their children's lives and many have developed special things to do.

- Remember that physical contact with your child is important from infancy. Don't be afraid.

- Write down, periodically, your feelings about being a parent and about how you "see" your child. You'll like looking back on your writings, and so will your child when he or she is old enough.

- Shower or bathe with your child when you come home from work or at bedtime, both to provide the child and yourself with pleasure and companionship and to give your spouse a little relief time.

- Give your time, rather than "things." Write out a list of activities you and your child enjoy sharing and let him or her choose one when a reward is in order.

- Remember to bring a memento home from each trip, if you travel, but be aware that it need not be an expensive present. The small soaps, cheap shower caps and shoe-cleaning cloths from hotels are always appreciated, as are airline magazines, plastic utensils from meals and packets of sugar or condiments.

Building self-esteem in the family

- Let each child do something alone with just one parent occasionally.

- Try to say at least one positive, affirming thing to your child every day.

- Try to provide an alternative pleasure for a younger child if an older one has something special planned. For example, if the older one is invited out to spend the night, a little one might be allowed to sleep in the sibling's bed.

- Let even very young children participate in family councils. Listen to them, and try to adopt their suggestions sometimes.

- Expect your children to do as much as they can, as well as they can, and let them know you do. But let them know that it's OK to make mistakes, too, and that mistakes — even Mom's and Dad's — show people ways to learn and improve.

Chapter 6

Family Heritage

Giving your child a sense of belonging to a special, important group — a FAMILY, large or small — is one of the nicest things you can do. One way of developing this sense is to help the child know all the members of the family and their relationships to one another — not always easy, the way some families are scattered today. Another is to observe family tradition. And then there's keeping track of it all....

BEING PART OF THE CLAN

Even when family members live nearby, children sometimes get confused about the relationships. Your efforts to give your child a sense of being a part of a clan will help give him or her a feeling of importance and a clearer self-image.

Understanding relationships

Who's who? Many families make it a point to discuss family relationships often: "Grandma is my mommy; Uncle Roger is Daddy's brother." And it's both instructive and fun to reminisce about family history and to talk about events currently going on.

- Put together a family of dolls or paper dolls to help a child understand relationships.

- Draw a family tree on shelf paper or paint one on a wall in your child's room and paste on photos of relatives.

- Devise different names for children to call two sets of grandparents in order to help distinguish them — Grandma and Grandpa for one set, for example, and Grammie and Grampie for the other. Or add surnames.

Some parents have the grandparents choose their own names.

- Use pictures to help acquaint children with relatives. Put together an album and look at it together often; give children photo cubes of their own. Or post pictures on the refrigerator or bulletin board.

"Relative" activities

Nothing can quite replace visits for getting to know one's relatives; if your family is one that enjoys big get-togethers on holidays or occasional huge family reunions, your children are especially lucky. Imaginative use of the telephone, the mail and the tape recorder can provide good substitutes for visits and gatherings, too.

- Let just one child at a time spend the night with grandparents if they live close by. The elders can serve a meal that the child especially likes, and the child can explore the grandparents' house and belongings and learn their routines.

- Give grandparents a photo album for pictures of their new grandchild and memorabilia such as first drawings. Ask them to write in the album about their memories. The visiting child will have his or her OWN book to look at over the years.

- Post photos of relatives near the phone so that children can see the relative they're talking to. Or make a telephone book for your child, using pictures, instead of written names, of relatives (and friends) he or she is most likely to want to call.

- Find the homes of faraway relatives on a map. Do a little research on their cities or countries and ask them to send pictures of their homes, gardens and neighborhoods.

- Or get a large, sturdy U.S. map puzzle and let a child carry around with him or her the piece representing the state a relative lives in.

- Let the children send special artwork to grandparents and cousins. They're apt to get mail back, which will make those family members very special.

- Encourage faraway grandparents to send notes, cards and inexpensive gifts by mail, often, instead of calling. Small children aren't usually able to carry on very interesting telephone conversations.

- Let your child add to your letters to relatives — a scribble, a picture and, later, a full signature. You can take dictation from the child, too.

- Tape spoken "letters" to relatives and mail the tapes back and forth.

- Consider joining a "Rent a Grandparent" program through a church or retired people's club if your child rarely sees any relatives.

TRADITIONS

Some traditions go back generations; others are begun when a new family is established and grows. A tradition can be as simple as the daily gathering at the dinner or breakfast table to share the day's events or as complex as a holiday celebration, including special menus and observances.

One thing to beware of is inflexibility in traditions. When one's outgrown, store it away in memory and let it go!

Birthdays

Some parents help small children keep track of the time before a birthday by describing it as so many "sleeps" away or by making a paper chain with the child and letting him or her tear off a link each day. For the little child to whom a year is an eternity, consider having "half birthdays," twice a year. And for the one whose birthday falls near a major holiday, select (with his or her help) another day for the party and some birthday presents.

- Join your child for lunch, if he or she is in a day care facility, and continue the practice when school's begun. Or let the child have lunch downtown or at work with a parent who works away from home.

- Plant a tree, shrub or perennial plant that the child selects, as a lasting memory of every birthday.

- Give your child a gift each year to add to a collection you start for him or her in early childhood — coins, bills, thimbles, small cars, and so on.

- Write a birthday letter to your child each year, noting highlights of the year, changes in the family and the child, special accomplishments of the child. The letters will become valuable keepsakes for him or her.

- Save the newspaper from the child's birthday each year to give him or her later.

- Ask the guests at the birthday party or family dinner to autograph the tablecloth with their names and the date; embroider the autographs or have the writers use colored pens. Use the cloth each year, adding new names and repeating the old. Or have guests sign on a white bedsheet, and later make it into a quilt.

- Burn a big decorative candle each year at the birthday party for the number of minutes that corresponds to the child's age.

- Transfer all the notes you've made to the baby book and put the year's pictures into the album — and share your child's year with him or her. (Forces you to organize, too!)

- Select a dull month in which there are no family birthdays and have an UNBIRTHDAY party every year, with UNBIRTHDAY presents for all (UNWRAPPED), an UNBIRTHDAY cake, games and songs.

Gift-giving holidays

- Begin the gift-giving season by letting the kids go through catalogs, marking items they like. You'll get a feeling for the kinds of things they want.

- Make felt Christmas stockings for your children and add a new design each year, representing something important to your child for that year. Symbols can range from a scrap of a school play costume, to a felt cut-out of an instrument the child has taken up, to a party favor.

- Take your children to a toy store before gift-giving holidays and let them pick out a toy to give to a less fortunate child, to teach them to enjoy giving as well as receiving.

- Have the children wrap gifts in their own artwork.

- Use those extra pictures you accumulate of everyone in the family as gift tags.

- Give Grandma and Grandpa a toy of the kids' choice on each gift-giving occasion. The toys remain at the grand-parents' home, to be played with only there — a permanent entertainment supply for visits.

- Let your children wake up Christmas morning with a cherry-red kiss from Santa imprinted on their foreheads.

- Give each child a Christmas tree ornament every year; store the ornaments separately and save for a treasured collection.

- Give your child certain types of gifts every year to make opening presents exciting: something to read, something to eat, something to play with outside, something snuggly to wear, something soft to take to bed. Or just three gifts (as Jesus received) — something special from Mom and Dad, something the child wants, and something he or she needs.

- Take a picture of your child playing with or wearing a gift he or she received from a relative or friend, and send it as a thank-you note to the gift-giver.

KEEPING RECORDS

The most important official record that parents must keep is their child's birth certificate. It's important to be sure the certificate is made out correctly and to keep it in a safe place, because you may need it when the child starts school, applies for a license or passport, and so forth. Many parents store one certified copy in a bank safe deposit box and keep others at home for use as needed.

Other records are important for your child's medical history. And still others, in the forms of diaries, tapes and photos, provide pleasant memories for a lifetime.

Medical and legal records

Some parents keep a notebook for each child, combining all medical, legal and school records. If advice and comments from doctors, dentists and teachers are included, the notebook can help to keep track of any recurring problems a child may have.

- Use the back of a copy of your child's birth certificate to record childhood diseases and their dates of occurrence.

- Or use recipe file cards for children's medical histories, noting illnesses, dates of vaccination and other information. The card can go with the child to camp or school and can be retained for a lifetime record.

- Carry a recipe file card in your wallet for each child so that you'll have it to make notes on at the doctor's office; transfer the notes to the child's permanent records at your leisure.

Written records for memories

- Use a calendar for a baby book if you don't want to keep a regular one. (Or buy a baby record book in calendar format.)

- Keep a pad and pencil handy to note milestones passed by your children. They can be entered in the baby books when there's time, and you won't have to depend on your memory.

- Keep notebooks of your children's great sayings to read from when they're a little older and to give them when they're grown up.

Spoken records

Tape recorders are as common in many homes today as radios and TVs are. We may be hesitant to use a tape recorder at first — our voices sound so strange — but, with a little practice, it becomes a valuable recording tool. Children usually love recording from the beginning.

- Consider taping "talks" that you have with your baby during feeding times. Review the day's events and the baby's progress and accomplishments. Save the tapes for future listening by the child.

- Tape record all kinds of family events, from ordinary dinner table conversations to family conferences and holiday celebrations.

- Let your child record a story he or she tells well, at various ages. The changes in voice and vocabulary will amaze you both, and you'll have a precious record of your child's voice, childhood delights and growth.

Records in pictures

Get good photos by moving in close to the child and by snapping quickly (babies and little children don't "hold it!"). Take lots of shots to assure yourself of getting some good ones. Keep backgrounds simple and uncluttered and get down to the child's eye level.

- Have a child hold the family pet or a favorite toy if he or she is embarrassed at picture-taking time.

- Take a semiannual picture of your child standing by a familiar piece of furniture or beside a parent whose hand rests on the child's head. Each half-year's growth shows up dramatically.

- Make photocopies of your child's hands at intervals.

- Trace your child's silhouette from a shadow every year or so.

Save Baby's First Shoes
**Preserve them by filling them with plaster of Paris
and later spraying them with gold,
silver or bronze paint.**

Chapter 7

Families on the Go

Today's families are part of a mobile society. They go out to work and play and shop, they travel on vacations, and about 25 percent of them move every year. Busy parents try to make each trip as enjoyable, convenient and safe as possible for themselves and the kids.

ERRANDS

Start out with a list of places you're going and things you're going to do, to make your trip as efficient and as short as possible. Pile library books, shopping lists and anything else to be taken along in a special place near the door, where you won't forget them.

Shopping with a small child — or with several — is no easy task. Many parents try to shop alone for big grocery orders, and some say they're able to save sitters' fees because of the careful comparison shopping they're able to do without the kids along. For older children, though, a trip to the store can be a learning experience in both nutrition and economy.

Saving trouble

- Get yourself dressed first in cold weather to avoid setting out with an already overheated, fussy baby or toddler.

- Keep a few disposable diapers in your car glove compartment . . . just in case. And tuck a packaged towelette and a plastic bag inside each, to make cleanup and disposal easy. Keep a box of diapers and towelettes at Grandma's house, too, for unplanned visits.

- Hook some large safety pins on your key chain — you might need them for diapers or quick clothing pin-ups.

- Change your baby in the open trunk of the car (with a blanket inside) or on the tailgate of a station wagon, instead of crouching uncomfortably in the back seat.

- Carry your child in a backpack while at a store, but watch out for quick-handed grabbing when you're near merchandise. If the child needs to walk a bit, free your hands by carrying your purse, the diaper bag and your purchases in the backpack.

- Use an adult's belt as a shopping cart "safety belt" for a toddler for both restraint and support.

- Bring toys and a pacifier, to which you have tied yarn or elastic, in your purse or pocket, and attach them securely to the shopping cart. Stuffed toys can wear cheap cat collars with yarn leashes. (Try this on the highchair, too; baby can "fish" for toys.)

- Give the kids something to eat, since the sight of food seems to beget a desire for it. Bring a snack or a whole lunch or buy something nutritious to eat or drink.

- Keep a metal shower curtain ring on the diaper bag and attach it to the handle of the grocery cart or stroller to free your hands.

- Save shopping altogether, when you can, by catalog shopping. You can compare prices in peace and quiet and save time, money and gas. And children love to browse through the catalogs, too.

Keeping tabs on kids

- Don't attach your child's name to clothing in an obvious place, say some parents, since a lost child is apt to respond positively to anyone who knows his or her name — and some strangers are dangerous.

- Get an expandable ID bracelet for your child which states name, address and phone number, and have him or her wear it ALWAYS.

- Ink a design on a helium balloon and attach the balloon to your child's wrist. Teach him or her to "pump" it if lost.

- Buy two balloons — one for each hand — to keep a child from grabbing and handling things.

- Dress a child who's not in a cart in bright-colored clothing (a red hat will do!) to keep track of him or her.

- Have a special family whistle or tune children can recognize and use to locate you if you get separated in a crowded place.

Involving the kids in shopping

- Turn your child into a mini-shopper. Give him or her a handful of box tops or coupons from products to match up with products you intend to buy. Or make up a grocery list in pictures for him or her to follow as you follow your own list.

- Take advantage of the opportunity to teach your child about nutrition, explaining why you buy some items and not others.

City travel with kids

- Set your baby's infant seat in the baby carriage when he or she is old enough to sit up and see what's to be seen while you walk.

- Use a baby harness if your toddler is tired of the stroller. If you embroider it or sew on appliqués, it will look more personalized ... less like a leash!

- Ride the subway in the front or back of a train, so that the kids can watch the tracks racing by.

- Let the children try to "guess" which stop is theirs so that they will learn their way around.

- Or, if they want to, let them sit a few seats away from you and pretend they are traveling alone. It makes them feel grown up, and they may pay more attention to the route.

Going to the Movies?

Take your toddler's booster chair and put it in the theater seat so he or she can see the screen without being in your lap — and be more comfortable, too. And when it's outgrown for home use, store it in the car trunk for unexpected movie outings.

TRIPS

Adults may be able to throw a few things into a bag and dash off, but when the kids are going along, things are different. It's easiest to travel with a child under six months — when he or she takes long naps — but with older children, thoughtful advance planning pays off. It's usually best not to talk about a trip with children very far ahead of time, in order to avoid unnecessary excitement. Try to arrange the timing of a trip so that everyone will arrive at the destination fresh and rested. Be sure to take along your pediatrician's telephone number.

Packing

It's hard to travel light with children. Clothing, food and toys take lots of space, but imaginative packing pays off. A backpack and/or an umbrella stroller are well worth any space they take up. Children enjoy selecting and packing the things they want to take. You'll need to set some limits as to types, sizes and number of toys that will be allowed, perhaps by sewing up drawstring "busy bags" that limit their choices of take-alongs. An old attaché case of Dad's might also be used.

- Simplify dressing for the whole family by designating specific bags for specific items: "Susie's clothes," for example, or the nighttime suitcase for the whole family. Put children's clothing on top for easy access if you're sharing suitcases.

- Use duffel bags for kids' clothes and toys — they'll fit more easily into the car or trunk.

- Save space by bringing inflatable toys. When not in use, they can be deflated and tucked away.

- Pack disposable diapers in the corners of suitcases to save the space a big box will take.

- Let the baby's quilt double as a changing pad if you're taking it along. Slip it in a pillowcase and tie a ribbon around it for easy carrying.

- Pack several large plastic bags. They can be used under sheets for the occasional bedwetter and for soiled laundry.

- Use a see-through lingerie case with zipper pockets and a hanger for small items for babies and parents. The bag is easily moved and hung, and the contents are visible.

- Take along a night light to reassure children waking in the night in a strange room.

- Pack a few of the baby's things that will make strange surroundings seem more like home — a crib sheet or receiving blanket that has been in the crib at home for a few days before the trip, a toy or two usually kept in the crib and a plexiglass mirror to put in the new crib so the baby can see himself or herself when waking up.

- Take along a few electrical outlet covers as a traveling childproofing measure if you'll be staying at a hotel or in the homes of others who might not have them.

- Take along a small pillow for a child to sit on and to use for naps en route and at the destination. It's also good for playing with toys in the lap.

- Tag special pillows, blankets and toys with your name and address so they can be returned if left somewhere.

- Carry a collapsible cup for the child too old for a bottle but too small to reach a drinking fountain.

- Keep plastic bandages and pre-moistened towelettes in the glove compartment of the car, or in a purse, pocket or carry-on bag if you're traveling by plane. Be sure you have plenty of medication along if anyone's using it.

- Consider renting at your destination a playpen or other needed equipment you can't take along.

Comfort in the car

Even if you travel in a large car or station wagon with plenty of room, you'll want to organize things so that they'll be easy to get at and not cause clutter.

- Make a slipcover for the front seat of the car with several pockets stitched to the side that will hang over the back for books, games and toys.

- Stuff a pillowcase with bulky cold-weather clothing. You'll have a pillow for napping, and the clothing will be in one place.

Peace in the car

Parents who travel a lot are used to children's initial excitement and restlessness in the car. The kids usually settle in after an hour or so, once territories and rules have been set.

- Travel at night, or get a very early start, so that the children will sleep in the car, but don't encourage so much sleep that you'll have well-rested, active kids at night when you're ready to rest.

- Put a small suitcase or box between two children in the back seat to clearly separate "sides."

- Place a firm-sided diaper bag filled with small toys and books between two toddlers in car seats. It can be reached easily by the children and holds enough to keep them busy for quite a distance. Stash some of the children's favorite toys and books in the bag well in advance of a trip so they will have more appeal.

- Make seating arrangements changeable. One adult in the back seat for all or half of a trip usually makes for pleasant riding.

- Stop often to run and play with the kids. You all need the break. Consider carrying a jump rope or a big, inflatable rubber ball for exercise and fun.

- Give the kids a five-minute warning before you stop so that they can put on shoes and sweaters or coats.

- Plan — and announce — a treat for the end of the day, so everyone will have something to look forward to: a swim in a motel pool, dinner at a restaurant, a pop stop.

- Take along earplugs for the adults!

Food in the car

If you carry an extra set of clothing for each child and a plastic bag for soiled clothes, a spill or an accident won't be a disaster. It's also a good idea to cover the back seat with a sheet or blanket; you can shake out the crumbs at rest stops. Keep packaged towelettes handy, or a squeeze bottle of water with a little liquid soap added. You can always use the spray from the windshield wipers, too, if you're all out of water for cleanups.

- Use an insulated six-pack bag to keep baby food warm or cold. Tape the baby spoon to one of the jars.

- Make things easy for yourself and substitute full jars of meat and fruit, for example, for half-jars of three or four foods.

- Pack instant baby cereal in separate small plastic bags or containers with powdered milk, and add warm water from a thermos or the hot tap of a sink when you're ready to feed the baby. Carry frozen baby food cubes or "plops" in a freezer chest, with your own juice popsicles for the older kids.

- Carry a supply of small paper plates with little slits in the center. Put the sticks of popsicles or ice cream bars through the slits and there'll be less mess on car seats and fingers.

- Hang a bagel for munching on a string pinned to a toddler's clothing or tied around a button or the car seat. There won't be many crumbs, and it won't fall on the floor.

- Fill several small plastic bags with an assortment of such treats as raisins, dry cereal and sunflower seeds, and bring them out when spirits need reviving.

- Take along a box of crackers and a tube of squirt cheese. The adult who's not driving can decorate the crackers with the cheese in designs, letters or numbers.

- Avoid taking very salty foods in the car — they call for lots of drinking and then for stops at restrooms.

- Cut sandwiches in different shapes for easy identification: triangles for those with mustard, rectangles for those with mayonnaise, for example.

- Make a mini-ice bucket out of a plastic pitcher. Put a container of yogurt or cottage cheese in among the ice cubes and the food will stay cold for a few hours.

Eating in restaurants

- Assemble your own "restaurant kit," with children's utensils, snacks, towelettes, a highchair strap or belt, small toys, and a small plastic clothespin, diaper pin or sweater guard to use to snap a napkin around a child's neck (better yet, a bib or two!). Make restaurant personnel happy by bringing a piece of newspaper to spread out under the highchair. Bring a cheap and easy booster seat — a couple of old catalogs wrapped in contact paper.

- Let someone walk around outdoors with an impatient toddler while you're waiting for the food to be served. Or let the child play with ice cubes on the highchair tray, or with paper napkins or straws.
- Consider wrapping snacks from home for your child in different kinds of food wrap — some, perhaps, even in colored wrapping paper. It will take lots of time to open all the "presents."
- Order a pot of hot water and extra napkins for cleanup and, perhaps, to wash a highchair tray that's not quite clean.

Drinks in the car

- Carry a thermos of cold water — it quenches thirst best. Add a little lemon juice for flavor.

- Hang canteens or wineskins filled with water or juice from the garment hook on each side of the back seat for children able to handle them.

- Make criss-cross slits in a baby bottle nipple; invert and secure it with the cap and cover on a plastic baby bottle filled with your toddler's favorite drink. Remove the cover and insert a straw when he or she wants a drink — no spills.

- Or put the liquids in well-washed plastic lemon or lime juice dispensers. (Remove the inserts with a sharp-pointed object, replace after filling and screw the caps back on.) If you freeze them before you leave, the drinks will stay cool as they melt.

- Satisfy both thirst and hunger with grapes. Oranges serve the same purpose, but they're messier.

- Freeze a half-full plastic container of water. When you're ready to go, fill the balance of the container with water for a long-lasting, cold thirst-quencher.

- Don't forget to take a cloth diaper or two to mop up spills — they're very absorbent.

Toys to take along

- Keep the toy supply in the trunk and bring out a few items after every rest stop, for variety, returning those in the car to the trunk.

- Tie toys to a child's car seat with short strings so that you won't have to pick them up constantly.

- Let the children fill school lunch boxes with small toys to play with — but not SO small that they can get lost in the car.

- Bring tiny toys that must go along in a shoe bag (closet-organizer). Keep it rolled up in the car; let it hang on a hotel room door.

- Wrap some favorite toys and new little surprises with plenty of string and tape. Unwrapping time will give you some peace, though you'll have some litter to clean out of the car.

Activities in the car

Check at your local library for books on games to play and songs to sing in the car. Keep a list of favorite songs and games in the glove compartment so you won't forget them when you suddenly need diversion.

- Tape greeting cards, pictures from magazines, even a swatch of a baby's wallpaper to the back of the front seat, so the car-seat rider will have something interesting to look at.

- Make a simple map even small children can follow as you drive in the car, with stops you're sure of marked.

- Put everyone's imagination to the test by "seeing things" in cloud formations.

- Store crayons, markers and coloring books in a metal cake pan with a sliding cover. The closed top provides a work surface. Avoid pencils and scissors — their sharp points may prove dangerous in case of a sudden stop.

- Buy magnetized games, or glue pieces of Velcro on board games and their playing pieces, to keep small parts from getting lost. For a dice game, put dice in a clear plastic jar so that you can just shake them, rather than roll and risk losing them.

- Take along a BIG catalog for the children to look at.

- Play tapes you've made of favorite stories and songs, or use tapes you've checked out from the library.

- Decorate a small paper bag with crayons. Tie the open end shut with a string and close the window on the string, with the bag outside. Instant car kite! You can do the same thing with a balloon.

Motion Sickness

- Keep a carsick-prone child on a high-carbohydrate, low-fat diet for a few days before a trip and go easy on liquids just before you go.
- Dress your child according to the temperature inside the car — being too warm may increase the chance of nausea.
- Have the child sit in the front seat or at least high enough in the back so that he or she can look out toward the front. The swiftly moving scenery to the side causes nausea.
- Make smooth starts and stops; drive slowly around curves to avoid unnecessary braking.
- Direct the child's attention to things outside the car and FAR OFF, rather than letting him or her focus on the shoulder of the road.
- Don't let the child do close work, such as reading or coloring.
- Have the child wear sunglasses to cut down glare.
- Avoid odors of strong-flavored foods or tobacco in the car.
- Open a window — fresh air often helps.
- When nausea is severe, have the child sit in a reclining position with eyes closed and head motionless.
- Carry a plastic ice cream container with a lid, or airline sickness bags, in case the child throws up.
- Try suspending a piece of chain (with wire) from the car's rear axle, so that it just touches the ground. This is the method truck drivers who pull loads of flammable liquids use to eliminate static electricity, which may cause nausea.
- Consider giving the child an over-the-counter drug for motion sickness — but remember that it will be effective only if taken BEFORE the trip.

Traveling by plane

Babies under two travel free, but you must inform the airline that you are traveling with an infant. Check with the airlines or a travel agent to determine the days of the week and the hours of flights which are least crowded so that you may be able to get an extra seat for the baby. (Remember that the trick of traveling at night by car, so the kids will sleep, doesn't necessarily transfer to air travel.) Try to reserve bulkhead seats (behind the first- and second-class dividers) to give you more leg room and space for your child to stand up and move about — or bassinet room, if you have a baby. Bassinets are available for your use behind the bulkheads, but should be arranged for when you reserve your seat. Try at least to reserve a seat on the aisle, for better mobility. Remember that you have limited storage space for carry-on luggage.

- Attach a luggage tag to your child's clothing, in case you get separated at the airport. Include the child's name and yours, your airline, flight number and immediate destination.

- Try to board the plane with a freshly diapered baby. There's little room for changing in an airplane restroom. Double-diapering is best — and cover with plastic pants. Carry a soft cloth diaper bag with a shoulder strap instead of a bulkier "boxy" bag. Fill it with more diapers than you think you will need, in case of the unexpected. Motion sickness bags are good for soiled diapers.

- Don't give your child a sugary snack before boarding; it will make him or her more active. You might even want to tire a wound-up child with a jog around the airport.

- Ask at the check-in counter if you may board early to avoid crowded aisles, and if you may carry on your umbrella stroller, if you wish to.

- Get a blanket and pillow from the overhead rack as you are being seated, to be sure of getting them.

- Carry a small infant in a front pack to avoid his or her slipping out of your arms and to free your hands while the baby sleeps. Some feel the front pack is safest for takeoff and landing — make sure the seat belt is over YOUR pelvis, not the baby's.

- Nurse your baby or give a bottle or pacifier at takeoff and landing, to reduce pressure on ears. Have gum or hard candy available for older children. Blowing up a balloon often helps older children, too. Teach children to "swallow" and "chew" and "yawn" to open Eustachian tubes. Make a game of facial motions for your baby. Even the crying some children do when their ears hurt helps equalize pressure imbalance. This is especially important if a child has a cold or allergies.

- Let a child old enough to do so carry his or her own "things" in a backpack.

- Bring a few new, SMALL toys and books and hand them out one at a time. A deck of cards is good. Be sure not to bring anything that could be dangerous if your child were to throw it. Some airlines supply "entertainment bags" if you ask.

- As you leave the plane, don't rush. Seasoned air travelers say leaving last is best with kids.

Food Fare

- Check with a flight attendant to find the best time to get his or her help with warming food or feeding a baby.
- Bring some food from home for your child. Airplane snacks are often nuts or crunchy things babies shouldn't eat, and you'll have something in case of delays. Cheerios are a good no-crumb snack.
- Let kids drink with straws — they're fun and they help prevent spills. Bring a tippee cup for a child too young to drink with a straw.
- Avoid cola drinks for children. Two or three have as much caffeine as a cup of coffee, and they'll make it hard for a child to sit still. They're also diuretic.
- Don't drink hot beverages while your child is in your lap; if they spill, your child may be scalded.

Traveling by train

A train trip can be a wonderful family experience. Kids can see the changing world and enjoy much more physical freedom than in a plane or car. The train becomes a traveling "home."

- Remember, when making reservations, that keeping the

family together in one compartment (first-class) will give you more control. However, if you travel in coach (second-class), you may ask the conductor to turn seats around to face each other.

- Ask about pillows and blankets after finding your seats if you're traveling in coach — temperatures on trains are not reliable. Dress in layers so clothes can be added or removed easily.

- Bring snacks or easy meals and drinks along — dining-car meals and items from snack carts may not be appropriate for your child. Ask food service people to warm bottles and baby food.

ENJOYING THE OUTDOORS

It's important to remember that children, even responsible preschoolers, must be watched constantly and extra carefully when you're in the woods or near water. Possibilities for fun and learning are there, however. Rainy-day puddles are as exciting as sunsets and wildlife.

Camping with kids

Roughing it with small children is not for everyone; if you're not sure you can take it, choose a campground with bathrooms, laundry facilities and a general store for your first outing. You may feel safer if your campsite is not near a road, lake or stream. As with any trip, accept each moment for its own enjoyment — original plans and destinations sometimes have to be modified.

- Stage a practice run in your backyard. You can test all your equipment and accustom your children to the experience.

- Include rain gear, boots and jackets when packing, no matter what the weather report says. Make washability a priority for camping clothes and select them with an eye to layering.

- Pack some clothing and gear in plastic pails of various sizes that you can use for dishwashing, hand laundry and grooming. A large plastic container with a lid makes a great "mini" laundry tub for little items. Just add a little soap, put on the lid and shake. The shaking is more efficient than swishing in a pail.

- Use empty plastic bread bags for soiled diapers and other wet items.

- Avoid the odors of damp, soiled clothing by packing fabric softener sheets in laundry bags.

- Use a small inflatable wading pool for a child's bathtub. You can add a quilt or pad and use it as a crib or playpen, too.

- Take along a backpack carrier so that you can carry a young child, but build up your "carrying time" before your trip. And pack a small mirror that you can use as a "rear view mirror" while you're hiking.

- Make up a "nature box," including books on birds, rocks and trees and plenty of plastic bags, jars and boxes to hold collections. Give the kids collecting "assignments": three leaves, five rocks, two pinecones.

- Pack a first-aid book and good first-aid kit, including supplies for hazards like insects, sun, cuts and bruises, and fever. Include a tweezers for the splinters that someone's sure to pick up.

- Bring empty plastic catsup or mustard containers to slip over tent stakes and prevent stubbed toes.

- Travel with food and drink in the car at all times, even if you plan to buy most supplies at your campground, so that you're prepared for anything.

- Consider taking along your own drinking water, if you don't trust the water at the campground. You DON'T want the kids to get diarrhea!

At the beach

- Remember that children burn much more easily than adults. Put hats on small children, and use a good sun block on their skin — products containing PABA are most effective.

- Use a big sheet for children to sit on instead of a blanket or towel. It's cooler, sand will shake off easily, and it will fold neatly and compactly for storage.

- Put beach gear, if there's a lot of it, into a plastic sled to pull across the sand.

- Or carry beach toys in a plastic laundry basket or mesh bag that you can dunk in the water for a quick rinse and drain at the end of the day.

- Mark your beach toys. Yours will probably look like everyone else's.

- Put large jar lids under the legs of a playpen, if you set it up at the beach, to keep them from sinking into the sand. (This works well in your yard at home, too.)

- Turn a playpen upside down over a blanket or sheet to keep the hot sun off a child and the child off the hot sand. Or open a large umbrella on a blanket.

- Remove diapers when giving a baby a swim. They absorb too much water and become very heavy so that the baby loses natural buoyancy.

- Fill a child's pail with water when leaving the beach and have the children dip their feet in it before entering the car.

- Or dust baby powder over children's sandy, dry arms and legs. Brush off powder and sand together.

Chapter 8

Child's Play

Child's play IS LEARNING, and many who have studied child development say that the more imaginative the play, the more a child may learn. Most parents have seen a child become more fascinated with the box a toy comes in than with the toy itself. This is not to say, "Don't buy toys," but to suggest that the fun and learning of play can depend upon what's at hand as well.

SEASONAL FUN

A climate like that of the South Sea Islands often seems like a dream come true to parents of active kids — warm weather, year 'round ... no mittens, caps, scarves, jackets .... Hardy souls in the north, though, enjoy the break between summer and winter activities.

Warm-weather specials

- Fill a flour shaker with cornstarch and let the kids sprinkle everything in sight outdoors. The first shower will clean things up.

- Let the kids draw on the sidewalk with colored chalk.

- Make a sandbox by setting an old tractor tire on the ground and filling it about half full of sand — there's plenty of seating space all around. Or use an old plastic swimming pool that will no longer hold water. Sink it into the ground and fill it with sand — the coarse kind, not the fine variety.

- Hang blankets over the clothesline to make a tent. Or set up a real tent for outdoor sleep-overs or naps.

- Attach a special baby swing to the older children's swing set so that they can all swing together.

- Put an old rubber doormat or a piece of indoor-outdoor carpeting under the swing to protect shoes and to keep some of the dirt outdoors.

- Let your child help you with garden chores, or give him or her a small plot to care for alone. Choose quick-growing things such as lettuce, beans, radishes, marigolds or bachelor buttons.

- Go miniature golfing with your child early in the morning, when it's cool. It's a child-sized play world.

Water play

- Put the baby bathtub, filled with water, under the baby's walker for kicking fun.

- Make a water pistol of an empty plastic detergent bottle or a kitchen baster.

- Put a plastic swimming pool at the bottom of the slide on a hot day and let the kids slide down into the water. (Don't buy a pool bigger than one adult can empty alone!)

- Fill balloons three-fourths full of water, close them with twist ties so they can be used again, and toss them around the yard.

- Give a child a dishpan of water, add detergent and let him or her whip up suds with an eggbeater. Then give the child a plastic straw or a spool to blow bubbles with.

- Let them paint the house with water and a big brush, or add food coloring to the water and let them paint the sidewalk.

- Make a very small hole in the bottom of a tin can, attach it to your child's tricycle and fill it with colored water. The child rides until the "gas" is gone.

- Fill a coaster wagon with water and add funnels, a kitchen baster and an eggbeater, for water fun without dirt. If you can stand the mess, a mudhole in the corner of your yard can surpass even a sandbox for children's delight.

- Let the kids wash the car. It may not be uniformly clean, but they'll have fun. Or let them wash trikes, bikes or toys.

Snowy-day specials

- Use an old plastic baby bathtub for a sled. (Punch a hole in the rim and attach a rope.) It won't go too fast, and the sides will keep a small child from falling out.

- Let a toddler use a dustpan for a snow shovel — right size, right height.

- Teach the kids to play a game of chase in the snow. Draw a big circle by shuffling through the snow and bisect it two ways, at right angles. The players can run only on the lines.

- Or show them how to make angels in the snow by lying down spread-eagled, moving arms up and down and legs together and apart.

- Fill a plastic squeeze or spray bottle with water to which you have added food coloring, so kids can draw on the snow or "paint" a snowman.

- Put special marks on a large outdoor thermometer to let children know when they must wear jackets, boots and other heavy clothing. (And also mark summer temperatures — when it's warm enough for picnics and water play.)

- Put a coating of petroleum jelly on kids' cheeks to protect them in cold or windy weather.

- Put inexpensive rubber gloves on over children's knit gloves to keep hands dry.

Too bad to go out

- Let the kids play with snow in the kitchen sink, or with LOTS of snow in the bathtub. Cover them up with raincoats worn backwards or outdoor play clothes. (This activity is best at floor-washing time — things might get messy.)

- Help kids with a little experiment: bring a bowl of snow inside and show them how little water it makes when it melts.

- Let the kids "skinny dip" in the bathtub for awhile before naptime or bedtime to get warm and sleepy.

INDOORS AND OUT

You can buy loads of expensive toys and equipment that are educational and fun for children to play with and you can take your children places where they'll learn a lot and have a good time. But you can also supply inexpensive things for them to play with which will provide hours of fun.

Playhouses, forts and such

- Drape a card table with an old sheet to make a playhouse that can be put up and taken down in minutes. Cut or draw windows and doors and let the kids decorate the sheet by drawing flowers, shutters and bricks with felt-tip pens.

- Use a large mover's carton or the big box from a household appliance for a playhouse. Cut doors and windows and let the children draw curtains, rugs and pictures inside and shrubbery, shutters and a doorbell outside. Remember that large cartons also make forts, tunnels, trains, boats — the only limit is the imagination.

- Cover the top of the old wooden playpen with a sheet of plywood and remove three or four slats from one side: instant playhouse.

- Hang bedspreads, sheets or blankets over chairs (hold them in place with spring clothespins) for a secret hideout.

- Make train or airplane seats for several children with chairs and stools from all over the house.

- Spread magazines or furniture cushions around the floor to make "rooms" and to use as stepping stones. Or use carpet squares for "magic carpets."

- Put an old mattress on the floor for tumbling and jumping to save wear and tear on chairs, couches and beds.

- Make a dollhouse by attaching together four boxes of the same size, two up and two down. Cut windows and doors. Give the kids scraps of cloth, wallpaper or carpeting and let them decorate.

Games

- Make a "busy box" for a toddler, with things to spin, a bell to ring, a lock and key, a chain to rattle, knobs and balls — all attached to a heavy cardboard box.

- Make an indoor sandbox out of any sturdy box or dishpan and fill it with used coffee grounds (hasten the drying process in the oven) — ideal for roads for little cars.

- Give an old shower curtain new life and map out on it, with a heavy felt-tip pen, a village full of roads and railroad tracks. The kids can spread it out and play with their cars and trucks and trains.

- Give a toddler an empty paper towel tube and a round balloon for a safe, easy-to-use baseball game. All kinds of tubes also make good tunnels for little cars.

- Make a ball stand for plastic bat-and-ball play by stacking two tennis ball cans. Kids have as much fun knocking over the cans as they do hitting the ball.

- Paint small, empty juice cans or eight-ounce plastic bottles and let the kids use them for bowling pins, with a small rubber ball.

- Get out the box of old clothes and let the kids play dress-up. Use old receiving blankets for capes, skirts and veils.

- Give children scraps of wrapping paper, tape and pieces of ribbon to play "birthday party," wrapping and tying their own toys for presents.

- Play dice games with little children, who find dice easier to handle than cards. You can make dice from art gum erasers cut in half and decorated with the usual dots or your own symbols.

- Let children who can't manage cards hold them with spring clothespins.

Playing Games with Children: Win or Lose?

Lose without "cheating" by using a handicap system that you devise. In checkers, for example, change sides every three moves. Or make a rule that no player can be more than one captured piece ahead.

Puzzles

- Glue small unpainted furniture knobs from the hardware store on puzzle pieces to make them easier for little children to handle. The knobs can be painted to match the pieces.

- Make puzzles by pasting large, clear pictures on heavy cardboard and covering them with clear contact paper. Cut with a matte knife or small saw into as many as 25 pieces, even for a preschooler, in distinctly different shapes — stars, triangles, arrows, circles, squares.

- Keep puzzles from getting hopelessly jumbled by marking the backs of all pieces of one puzzle with one color, another puzzle with a different color, and so on. They will be easier to sort by color on the back than by design on the front.

Things to "unmake" and "undo"

- Remember that any appliance or gadget on its way to the trash pile offers fascinating possibilities for unscrewing, opening and taking apart, even smashing.

- Check out garage sales for broken clocks, record players or cameras.

- Let the kids participate in any dismantling project in house or yard — a wall being taken down, a garden dug, a sidewalk being broken up.

Cleaning and repairing toys

- Save work by buying machine-washable stuffed toys and dishwasher-safe plastic toys.

- Clean and deodorize toys by wiping them off with a moist cloth dipped in baking soda.

- Shake stuffed toys in a bag with generous amounts of cornmeal. Brush out the cornmeal, and the dirt will come with it. Cornstarch or baking powder will work as well.

- Or use rug shampoo and a brush to clean stuffed toys.

- Clean cloth dolls by making a paste of soap flakes and water, applying it with a toothbrush, and wiping off with a damp cloth.

- Paint clear nail polish over the ceramic face of a doll to freshen it. And paint paper dolls with nail polish to keep them from tearing.

- Apply two or three coats of nail polish to pinholes in inflatable toys.

- Soak plastic toys that have gotten out of shape in hot water, then work them back into shape.

- Tape strips of masking tape over the corners of boxes of games and puzzles BEFORE they break. And preserve board games, puzzles and even book covers with generous coats of spar varnish, clear polyethylene paint or clear contact paper. All will make the items easy to clean.

- Cut circles from a wooden broom handle; sand and paint them to replace lost checkers.

ARTS AND CRAFTS

Don't ask your beginning scribbler or sculptor, "What is it?", say those who work with children in arts and crafts. Such a question puts a child on the spot. Instead, talk about colors, thickness or thinness of paint, interesting shapes. Save trouble when messy work is to be done by having your child wear an adult's old shirt with shortened sleeves. You save more trouble if you have a tiled floor or put down a plastic rug runner or piece of linoleum in the kids' "creative corner." Covering the work table with an old sheet also makes cleanup easy.

Painting

Investigate free or inexpensive sources of interesting kinds of paper: rolls of discontinued black-and-white wallpaper for coloring; shelf paper; ends of rolls of newsprint from your local newspaper; brown paper bags; even newspaper want-ad pages, on which print is dense enough to paint over. Save diaper boxes with white interiors and cut them up for painting on. Or make a writing or coloring board by covering a piece of cardboard with clear contact paper. Erase with a dampened tissue or paper towel.

- Make finger paint for kids with water or canned milk and food coloring.

- Or, combine shaving cream or even pudding with food coloring and let your child paint on the shiny side of freezer paper, for gooey fun.

- Or let your child finger-paint with shortening on cookie sheets.

- Buy powdered water colors and mix only the amounts needed, in small jars or foam plastic egg cartons.

- Mix powdered paint with liquid starch instead of water to get a better consistency for beginning painters.

- Or make instant paint by adding a few drops of food coloring to a little liquid starch in a small container.

- Mix a little egg yolk, dry detergent and food coloring to make a paint that will stick to a shiny surface such as glass, foil or freezer paper.

- Use an ashtray with cigarette rests and double-suction disks underneath as a water dish — it provides a place to rest a brush and won't tip.

- Insert water or paint containers into holes you've cut in a big synthetic sponge to prevent tip-overs and to soak up overflow.

- Mix a little detergent with finger paints or tempera paints to make cleanup easy.

- Save trips to the sink for hand cleanup by putting some paper towels and a spray bottle filled with water on the work table.

Brushes

- Let beginners paint with pastry brushes, which pick up a lot of paint. Or let them use cotton swabs or pipe cleaners with ends twisted into loops for painting that doesn't require fine line work.

- Get toddlers' brushes from the hardware store. Brushes used for painting trim are wide enough and short-handled enough for them.

- Fill a cleaned-out roll-on deodorant bottle with paint and let the kids roll paint on.

Recycling crayons

- Sharpen crayons by dipping them in hot water and rolling them to a point between your thumb and forefinger.

- Make "double color" crayons by removing the paper from two of the same length, melting one side of each over a candle flame and letting them dry together. Or bind three or four different color crayons together with a rubber band.

- Melt old crayons of the same color (with paper removed) in empty juice cans set in hot water over medium heat on the stove. Pour the wax into the cups of an old muffin tin, cool and unmold — fun crayons for young children.

Glue

- Use liquid starch as glue for kids. It works well on tissue paper collages, cut-outs, overlays or assembly work and it dries overnight.

- Use up old clear nail polish as glue; the little brush is a good size for a child. Refill the empty bottle with glue, too.

- Put glue in one section of a foam plastic egg carton and the small items to be glued — macaroni, beans, rice, whatever — in other sections.

- Keep paste fresh and smooth by adding a few drops of water to it before closing the jar.

- Lubricate the cap grooves of glue and paste containers with petroleum jelly for easy opening and closing.

Storing materials

- Install a café curtain rod as a dispenser for a big roll of shelf paper for children's drawing and painting activities. Hang a pair of blunt-nosed scissors nearby so that children can help themselves.

- Use a kitchen cutlery tray to store art supplies and keep them separated.

- Poke holes in a block of styrofoam with one colored marker and stand markers all up in the block to keep them together and visible for color selection.

- Store crayons in washed plastic containers from fast-food burgers when boxes are torn or smashed.

- Store felt-tipped pens in sealed jars to keep them from drying out.

Preserving drawings

- Preserve a crayon drawing by putting it faceup on the ironing board (with newspapers underneath to protect the pad) and laying over it a piece of cotton sheeting. Iron the fabric firmly at a low to medium setting until the drawing has been transferred to the cloth, and let it cool before moving it.

- Spray drawings with hair spray to preserve the paper and keep the colors from rubbing off.

- Or soak drawings in a solution which, it has been claimed, will give them "an estimated life of 200 years." Dissolve a milk of magnesia tablet in a quart of club soda and let it sit overnight. Soak the paper in the solution for an hour, pat it dry and don't move it until it's completely dry.

Your "artist" on display

Save artwork YOU like; let the kids keep the things THEY like; and encourage throwing away pieces no one especially likes. You'll cut down on the quantity of "keepers," and you'll be helping your children be more critical of their own work. Your praise will be believable, too.

- Let the children write notes to their grandparents on the backs of drawings, saving paper as well as getting the artwork out into the world where it will be appreciated.

- Let them make gift wrap by decorating white shelf paper with crayons or paints.

- Take pictures of your child standing by a display of his or her work posted on the refrigerator with magnets or displayed somewhere else. Later you can all look back and see the fine things that were done.

- Use a big piece of cardboard as a bulletin board to hang paintings on when the refrigerator door is full.

- Attach drawings to painted surfaces with dabs of toothpaste on the four corners.

- Show your appreciation of a child's artwork by hanging a piece in the LIVING ROOM in a frame with an easily removable back. Change the artwork frequently.

- Make placemats of drawings or paintings by sealing them between two layers of clear contact paper. Or insert them in plastic folders for changeable placemats.

- Use a clear plastic tablecloth and display drawings under it. Or, if you have glass-covered tables, slide artwork between glass and tabletops.

- Let kids paste drawings on formula cans, coffee cans or other cans with plastic lids. They make great gift containers and are reusable as containers for art supplies and other small objects.

- Punch holes in drawings and save them in loose-leaf notebooks. Or let kids save the drawings they want by clipping them together with giant, colored plastic clips.

GETTING READY FOR SCHOOL

The decision to send a child to nursery school is an individual one, determined by personal preference, family finances, availability of playmates and other factors. Those who LIKE the idea of nursery school say it helps prepare children for kindergarten and helps them learn to relate to adults other than their parents and adjust to the company of other children. Those who DON'T like the idea feel that with a little effort they can provide appropriate learning experiences at home and, often, that they just aren't ready to let their children go.

Organizing for school

- Set the school-night bedtime before school starts and begin to stick to it. Get up early yourself and get things going on the morning schedule you'll follow on school days.

- Get school clothes together and involve the child as much as possible in the selection of new ones.

- Start the routine of selecting and laying out the next day's clothes the night before, including shoes and socks. Have your child begin the habit of dressing completely before breakfast.

- Walk to school or the bus stop with your child several times. Discuss the best ways to get there and talk about any dangers along the way, such as busy intersections.

- Draw a big map including the home-to-school route and put in major landmarks. Let your child play on it with small cars or dolls.

- Talk a lot about what school will be like, but be careful not to promise anything you're not sure will happen. Listen carefully to your child to discover fears and worries he or she may have. Try to put yourself in the child's place if some fears seem silly to you — they're very real to him or her.

- Rehearse your child in reciting his or her full name, address and phone number.

- Try role-playing, and let the child play both pupil and teacher.

- Give your child two gifts to help him or her with scheduling: an alarm clock — and start setting it for bedtime and wake-up time — and a calendar on which he or she can mark and cross off special days.

Learning Left from Right

A child can form the letter L by holding up the left hand, fingers together and thumb stuck out straight ... and learn two things at once. Or, if the child is right-handed, he or she "writes with the right."

Off-to-school routines

It's usually helpful to a child to let him or her visit nursery school or kindergarten and meet the teacher before the first day, if possible. Many schools have a "get acquainted" day or open house to which both parents and pupils are invited — if your school does, try not to miss it.

- Set a timer to help your child know when it's time to gather belongings and get ready to leave for school.

- Attach name tags to any clothes that will be removed at school — sweaters, jackets and such.

- Supply your child with an empty paper towel tube for carrying important papers to and from school. In rainy weather, the tube can be slipped into a plastic bag for extra protection.

- Or get the child a regular school bag or small backpack — either is very grown-up. (And a backpack won't wear out from being dragged on the ground, as a bag will.)

- Keep old diaper pins handy to pin notes to the teacher on the child's clothing.

- Let Dad drop your child at school the first few days, if he's the one who usually goes off to work. The child will be accustomed to saying goodbye to him and it won't be so hard.

- Be sure your child understands that no one but a parent (or other designated person) can pick him or her up from school without written permission.

- Don't forget to inquire each day about school activities. Listen very carefully to the answers in order to head off any problems. (Some children will share more than others; don't give your child the "third degree"!) You may find that the best time to ask about the day's events is at night, as you are tucking your child into bed.

Chapter 9

Special Situations

The topics of the first eight chapters of this book apply to parents and children in general. The sections in this chapter apply to those whose situations are a "little bit different," in one way or another. Here are the tips of parents who have been in these special situations and who have learned the best ways — for them, at least — of dealing with certain circumstances.

CESAREAN DELIVERIES

If you know you'll be having a C-section, you can make some decisions before you go to the hospital. If you want the father to be present, request your doctor's permission. It may be the anesthesiologist who makes the decisions, but you'll work through your own doctor. Request minimal, local medication, if you want that. Plan to nurse the baby immediately after the anesthetic has worn off, if the baby will be breastfed. Rooming-in may be available, or you may ask that the baby be brought to you for feeding on demand. Many prepared childbirth groups offer C-section classes.

When you get home

- Stay in bed as much as you can. Keep the baby in a bassinet or another small bed at your bedside, with a good supply of diapers and baby clothes handy.

- Get a robe that buttons all the way down the front. You'll find getting into and out of it easier than stepping in and out of one that opens only part way down.

- Wear a protective panty girdle to keep loose clothing from rubbing on your tender incision.

- Use a hair dryer to dry your incision thoroughly after a bath to prevent the pain of rubbing the tender area with a towel.

- Put a pillow in your lap when nursing, both to support the baby and to protect your incision.

- Try making a playpen of your bed, if you must care for a toddler, too. Keep toys and books within reach.

Caring for tender abdominal muscles

- Use your foot as a lever to raise a toddler up to you when you are in a chair or in bed, rather than leaning down to lift him or her from the floor.

- Use a high changing table, not a bed, to avoid bending down when you dress the baby.

- Try to avoid holding the baby in one arm while you work around the house, until your muscles are stronger. Consider using a mechanical swing if the baby is fussy and wants attention.

- Don't vacuum for a couple of months — the particular movements involved are hardest on abdominal muscles. It's a good job for a father or another family member to take over.

National Organization

The aim of Cesareans/Support, Education and Concern (C/SEC) is to make a cesarean delivery a good and meaningful experience for families. Printed materials offered include a newsletter, guides, pamphlets and manuals. Write C/SEC at 66 Christopher Road,Waltham, MA 02154 or call 617-547-7188.

TWINS

"Help!" is the first cry of parents of multiples. And help of every kind is what's needed, right from day one. Your friends, neighbors or relatives may offer — don't be too proud to accept. Remember that it's very important to make time for yourself, even to the point of going away for a weekend if that's the only way you can do it.

A hospital nurse or your doctor may be able to put you in touch with your local twins' clubs. The benefits of belonging are MULTIPLE!

Equipment

- Get only about one-and-a-half times the number of everyday items for twins that you'd have for a single baby — diapers, sleepers, undershirts, bibs, sheets and plastic pants — especially in the very small sizes that are quickly outgrown. Ask for "twin discounts" if they're not offered; many stores will give them.

- Beg, borrow or buy two of some basic pieces of equipment such as car seats, highchairs (folding ones are good for travel and save space at home) and playpens. You'll be able to get by with one crib for a few months, putting one baby at each end. (But you may find that they scoot around in order to be next to each other, seeking their prenatal environment.)

- Use wind-up swings to substitute for your cuddling when you're busy, or to quiet fussy or overtired babies. You'll find the seats helpful when you travel or go visiting with the twins, too.

- Consider forgetting playpens altogether and turn the twins' room into a more comfortable and convenient play space. Put an expanding gate on the door so you can keep the kids in and still look in on them. Childproof carefully!

- Investigate the usefulness FOR YOU of the twin strollers available. On sidewalks in town, small wheels that swivel give good maneuverability, but you'll need large wheels for areas without sidewalks. A tandem-type double stroller will be easier to get through doorways and store entrances than a side-by-side model. You may be able to find a clip with which you can attach two single strollers, and later, you may wish to push one twin in a single stroller and back-pack the other.

Telling one from the other

- Put nail polish on a toenail of one twin to help you tell identicals apart.

- Color code diaper pins, or tie different colored ankle ribbons on the twins.

- Or dress them in different colored clothes — one always in red, the other in blue. (They'll probably object to wearing the same color all the time when they're older, but you'll be past the critical point by then.)

- Put a bracelet on one. Or snip a bit of one's hair.

- Keep the shoes of toddler twins separate by lacing one pair OVER, the other UNDER, in the two bottom holes. Or tie a knot in the center of one twin's shoelaces.

Feeding two

- Note which breast you used for the last feeding of each twin, if you're nursing, and switch sides for each feeding to encourage the babies' eye muscle control.

- Use small bottles for feeding when the babies are little. Twins are usually smaller than other babies and take less at each feeding.

- Avoid filling up your refrigerator with bottles by making up formula as you need it, as you would instant coffee. Or make a big batch and store it in a large sterilized bottle. If you make it double strength, you can add boiling water to warm it to room temperature.

- Bottle-feed two hungry babies at once in infant seats on the floor — but be sure to make yourself comfortable before you start.

- Give yourself a little time to prepare a meal by putting twins about four months old in highchairs with blanket rolls on both sides to brace them. Put special bottle straws in their bottles and let them suck away.

- Save time and energy by feeding both twins with the same spoon from the same bowl (or right from the jar) when they're ready for solids. They're bound to share most germs, anyway.

- Save time by feeding the morning cereal in the twins' bottles, with nipples cut larger. You can continue this easy practice even when you're spoon feeding other meals.

- Feed the babies lunch and dinner before the rest of the family until they can handle eating alone well. You deserve and need an undisturbed meal AT LEAST once a day.

Daily routines

When the twins are tiny you'll find it easier to keep them on the same schedule, even if it means waking one for a feeding. Put them down for naps at the same time from the beginning in order to establish a routine which gives you a little time for yourself.

- Don't try to bathe two tiny infants at once; it's better to have one screaming in the crib than two screaming in the tub.

- Keep charts at the ends of the babies' cribs to record feedings, stools and baths and save confusion and mixups.

- Try to have a sitter with you occasionally to help. When you leave your twins with a sitter, you'll probably prefer a mature, experienced person; consider having two teenage sitters to share the duties if an older person isn't available.

- Take comfort when both babies scream at the same time — it almost always means that it's just "crying time" and that there's nothing really wrong with either.

- Once the babies can crawl or walk, sit down on the floor and let them come to you for cuddling without lifting them up and putting your back in jeopardy.

- Don't be surprised if your twins are a bit slow in talking (or in any other aspect of development). If they were preemies, you may want to think of them in terms of their gestational (anticipated birth) age rather than their chronological age. And remember that they have each other; they may not NEED to talk.

- Train yourself never to yell at your twins, or you'll be yelling twice as much as other mothers. And resign yourself from the beginning to the fact that most things take twice as long to do. You don't want to bring up children who are always rushed.

- Speak clearly and distinctly to EACH twin, and wait for EACH to answer, to help avoid the development of a special language that only they will speak and understand and to be sure that one doesn't start to answer for both.

- Childproof your home extra carefully. What one pair of eyes doesn't see, the other surely will.

National Organizations

An annual convention, meetings and a newsletter are offered by the National Organization of Mothers of Twins Clubs, in addition to information about local clubs throughout the country. Reach the organization at 5402 Amberwood Lane, Rockville, MD 20853 (301-460-9108). The Center for the Study of Multiple Birth acts as a clearinghouse on twin research, operates a bookstore, assists parents with special problems and provides information for the media. Contact the center at 333 East Superior Street, Suite 463-5, Chicago, IL 60611 (312-266-9093).

Treating twins "like other kids"

- Avoid any implications, right from the beginning, that your twins are a "matched set." Use their names, instead of calling them "the twins," encourage separation sometimes and don't ALWAYS dress them alike. Encourage other-than-twin nicknames as they grow older.

- Be careful not to make remarks before your twins, even when they're tiny, about their being "double trouble" and "twice the work," and don't allow others to do so.

- Try to treat twins even-handedly and to be sure you know which one is "dominant." The twin who seems to be the "passive" one may effectively manipulate the other and get his or her own way most of the time.

- Be sure to take individual pictures of the twins. They will probably need baby pictures for school someday, and a picture of oneself alone helps build self-esteem.

- Provide two birthday cakes, especially as twins get older.

- Be aware that identicals often need more togetherness than fraternal twins, but as they grow, try to interest them in different activities and separate them sometimes.

ADOPTED CHILDREN

Parenthood is the ongoing process and responsibility of caring for a child. Whether the child is biologically yours or adopted, your job as a parent is the same. While adoption doesn't allow you the nine months of anticipation usually allotted by a pregnancy, be aware that those nine months don't allow a "birth" parent to be fully prepared for the unanticipated demands of parenthood, either!

From the beginning

- If you have not been a birth parent yourself, you might wish to make arrangements to tour the obstetrical department of a hospital and learn about prenatal care so you will be completely comfortable with the idea of birth.

- Ask those with whom you work at the agency to suggest books about adoption for both adults and children. Helpful workshops and other services may also be available through the agency.

- Let your child know from the beginning that he or she came into the family by adoption, but talk a great deal more about your family relationships than you do about the adoption process.

- Avoid using sugar-coated clichés that make things seem unnaturally rosy and set your child apart as special. "We chose you from all the others" is one such cliché.

- Don't make a practice of celebrating the day your child came into the family — more than one "birthday" makes a child different from others and may embarrass him or her.

- Help give your child roots, if you can, by showing the child the hospital and town in which he or she was born and the building which houses the agency through which adoption was arranged.

- Obtain as much information about your child's biological parents as you can and share with the child realistic details about their looks and sizes, hobbies, talents and interests.

- Let the child participate in the formal adoption procedure in ways appropriate to his or her age, "signing" with you if possible and taking part in other activities.

- Help another child accept the entrance of the child into the family by participating in the complete procedure as much as possible, and use terms such as "your brother (or sister)" and "our family" consistently.

- Include your extended family and close friends in the celebration of adoption as you would at a wedding or christening. If you can arrange to have the judge who authorized the adoption at your home for the affirming festivities, so much the better.

Adopting a child from a foreign country

While a child of another race will become a true member of your family, he or she can never be fully assimilated — it's cruel and unrealistic to let such a child think he or she is "just like you." The more thoroughly you are able to familiarize yourself with such things as the other country's religion and holidays, social mores and family relationships, the better you will be equipped to help your child retain his or her cultural identity and racial pride. As marriage may bring new cultural dimensions to a family, so may the adoption of a child from abroad.

- Don't allow yourself to be discouraged if your child seems less than perfectly healthy when he or she arrives. Most illnesses are treatable and reversible, and seeing your child through to full health can deepen your bonds with each other.

- And don't worry if he or she seems behind in development. Undernourishment and the understimulation of life in an orphanage may be responsible, and both can be corrected.

- Put off a visit to a doctor for at least 24 hours after your child's arrival — the testing and handling necessary in a checkup are liable to be frightening. And delay dental care or elective medical procedures, if at all possible, until your child is adjusted to your family (and the language, if he or she is talking).

- Try to maintain a loose, relaxed schedule for a time; children from some cultures live unstructured, flexible lives, especially in regard to eating and sleeping.

- Respect your child's habit of sleeping with an adult or another child when he or she first arrives, if that has been his or her pattern and you can manage it.

- Expect some behavioral changes in toddlers and pre-schoolers—regression in toilet training, increased irritability, fearfulness, sleep problems, aggressive behavior. They're all natural reactions to a changed life.

- Let your child keep any security items he or she may have brought along, even if they don't meet your standards of cleanliness or appropriateness.

- Discuss milk intolerance with your doctor, if your child shows signs of it. Children from many cultures have difficulty tolerating milk and suffer from cramps and diarrhea if they are given it.

- Allow your child contact with other children from his or her own land and culture, if possible, especially if he or she is old enough to talk.

Adoption Directory

THE NATIONAL DIRECTORY OF INTERCOUNTRY ADOPTION SERVICE RESOURCES, published by the U.S. Department of Health and Human Services, lists 400 agencies and organizations that handle overseas adoptions. To order, send $6.50 to the Superintendent of Documents, U.S. Government Printing Office, Washington, DC 20402.

SINGLE PARENTS

A dependable support system is essential for a single parent. It's not a sign of weakness to seek support; in reality, it's a sign of strength to be able to admit that you can't do everything, be everything, all alone. Your support may come from family members, friends-turned-into-extended-family or established support groups. If you have no one with whom you can discuss your feelings and frustrations, seek professional help through an agency you can locate in your yellow pages or a friend's recommendation.

Try to look on the bright side of single parenting. Some of the things that could be considered disadvantages can be thought of as advantages. For example,you have to make all the decisions, but you can make the ones you WANT and THINK RIGHT. And your child may well turn out to be more responsible, helpful and independent than some of those with two parents.

If you're a divorced single parent, be careful not to ask your child to be a messenger between parents, however much you may be tempted to do so, and don't pump the child for details of the other person's life.

Divorced parents, with custody

Even though you and your spouse may not be able to get along, remember that your children need two parents. Parents should strive for basic agreement in general matters of child rearing so they don't undermine each other's efforts.

- Expect some behavioral changes in toddlers and pre-schoolers — regression in toilet training, increased irritability, fearfulness, sleep problems, aggressive behavior. They're all natural reactions to a changed life.

- But be aware that your child's problems will more often than not be normal development phases, due neither to the divorce nor to the single parent situation.

- Be sure your child understands that he or she is not responsible in any way for the divorce. You cannot repeat this too often!

- Give your child more of your time, if it seems necessary, but not ALL your time. You need your own hobbies and friends.

- Be open with your child about any changes in financial conditions.

- Eat out as often as your budget allows. You need the break and your children do, too.

- Don't try to continue holiday routines as usual. Bring in new people, start new traditions. Try a special new holiday location, if you can.

Visiting your child

- Try to visit in different places — the custodial home, where your child can play host; restaurants; your own home; places you go together.

- Don't rule out having others present during visits, but don't ALWAYS include another person; you and your child need time alone together.

- Visit with your child as often as possible. Sharing a regular weekly lunch is one way.

- Keep visiting schedules somewhat flexible to avoid disappointment and uncertainty. Give full, honest explanations to your child if you must cancel or postpone a visit.

- Try to do some things with your child by phone, if you can't visit as often as you'd like (obviously easier if no tolls are involved). You might arrange to watch a TV show "together" and discuss it by phone, to listen to a radio program the same way or to read together over the phone.

Support Groups for Single Parents

Parents Without Partners International, 7910 Woodmont Avenue, Bethesda, MD 20814, (202-654-8850) is devoted exclusively to the welfare and interests of single parents (custodial and noncustodial; widowed, divorced or never married) and their children. A monthly magazine is included in membership. Big Brothers/Big Sisters of America, 117 South 17th Street, Suite 1200, Philadelphia, PA 19103, are agencies that work with fatherless boys and motherless girls.

STEPPARENTING

Some 20 million American adults are stepparents. The "move-in" parent is usually the one who must be most willing and able to adjust to established routines and patterns. He or she must try to know all the rules, considerations and conditions before taking on the new role — and be prepared for them all to change.

The parent who leaves his or her own children and subsequently assumes care and responsibility for stepchildren often fights useless guilt and may unconsciously withhold affection from the stepchildren.

Those who have gone through the stepparenting experience say real adjustment may take several years, but that it's all well worth the effort.

First meetings

- Make the first meeting with prospective stepchildren casual, not a formal appointment which requires elaborate preparation.

- Meet on neutral territory — a restaurant or park, perhaps — and have a specific plan for an activity. Making conversation may be difficult; doing something fun probably won't.

- Don't bring gifts to a first meeting (unless it's a birthday party!), to avoid the look of bribery.

Living as a new family

- Don't surprise your children with a new marriage and/or a new house; keep them informed. Avoid wild enthusiasm and admit that there will be problems, which you'll all work to solve.

- Start your new family in a new house or apartment, if it's AT ALL possible (and especially if more than one set of children is involved), in order to cut down on feelings involved with territory.

- Don't expect instant love to develop between stepchildren and stepparents, or between step-siblings, just as you don't expect it with a new baby. Move slowly and let caring develop over a period of time.

- Let all the children participate in deciding what the stepparent will be called. Some want to move right to Mommy/Daddy, for a secure family feeling; others don't. First names may work best, or nicknames may be invented.

- Refer to your stepchild as "our son" or "my daughter" when the occasion arises, rather than as your stepchild. This is hard at first, but it's basic to a good relationship.

- Discuss adopting the stepchild, if it's being considered, WITH the child. Taking the new family's name may offer security to some children, but others may wish to retain their original names. Grandparents may also have wishes you want to consider.

- Let the biological parent do as much of the disciplining of a child as possible at first — share it gradually. This is an especially tricky challenge for a stepmother, who may spend more time with a child than the father does.

- Talk about rules, limitations and unfamiliar parenting situations with your spouse. Discuss disagreements in private so children won't feel a sense of insecurity and uncertainty.

The visiting child

- Make sure the visiting child (and any who live there) understands that it's his or her HOME, too.

- Assign the child a room alone, if possible, or at least a closet, shelf or drawer for his or her possessions, which will remain undisturbed between visits.

- Give the child a place at the table that's not makeshift, so he or she won't feel like an intruder.

- Allow the visiting child a few days to settle in on a long visit before starting a round of activities.

- Include the child in household chores and projects as well as in excursions and play, to help him or her feel a part of family life and to make the other children accept the visitor as one of the family.

- Provide for some time alone together for the visiting child and his or her natural parent. This may on occasion actually involve a stepparent's going away for a few hours or a day or two.

- Save the BEST — be it a gift or an activity — for last, so a visit ends on a high note.

- Lay some plans SOMETIMES for pleasant activities for the next visit before a child leaves so there will be something to anticipate. Making a point of ALWAYS doing this, however, is unnatural and may make children who live in the home permanently feel jealous.

National Organization

The Step Family Foundation, Inc., 333 West End Avenue, New York, NY 10023 (212-877-3244) will provide information on regional groups. The group organizes lectures and workshops and publishes a newsletter.

LEFT-HANDERS

In Grandma's day it wasn't unusual to hear that the right hand was the "angel's hand" and the left the "devil's hand." Few people today are so thoughtless, but right-handed parents might look closely at such tools as ladles, butter knives and can openers — and even certain toys — before they label left-handed children awkward. A left-handed child may be encouraged to try doing some things, such as eating, right-handed, in order to save trouble for himself or herself later, but DON'T PUSH IT!

- Don't make such a big deal of a child's being a lefty that he or she feels handicapped. Making a point of always seating the child at the end of the table, for example, draws unnecessary attention to him or her and sets up a habit that can't always be followed.

- Provide left-handed scissors from the start, because right-handed ones simply don't work very well for a lefty. And check to be sure that your child's school provides them, or send your own.

- Suggest that the child turn right-handed scissors upside down, if he or she MUST use them sometimes.

- Tilt paper to the right instead of the left when your left-handed child begins to draw and write, to avoid awkward and often inconvenient "hooked hand" writing later.

- Teach your lefty to cross the left-hand string over the right in order to get a straight bow.

- Try having a left-handed child follow your movements in the reflection of a mirror when he or she needs to imitate some action of yours to learn a new skill.

- Buy some special left-handed equipment to make your child's life easier and to add a little humor — a mug with the child's name on the front and the handle on the left, a notebook that opens from the back, a left-handed baseball mitt, a "lefty" T-shirt. There are special left-handed merchandise shops in many cities, and some mail order catalogs offer left-handed items.

Index

Order Form

Name _____

Address _____

City _____ State _____ Zip _____

Please charge my ☐ Visa ☐ Mastercharge Account

Accnt. # _____ Exp. Date _____

Signature _____

Your group or organization may qualify for group quantity discounts: please write for further information to Marjie Cargill, Meadowbrook Press. 18318 Minnetonka Blvd., Deephaven, MN 55391

Quant.	Title	Cost Per Book	AMOUNT
		Total	

We do not ship C.O.D. Postage and handling included in all prices.
Check or money order payable to Meadowbrook Press.

Meadowbrook Press

18318 Minnetonka Boulevard • Deephaven, Minnesota 55391

Dept DM/PPT